HOPES FOR SCHOOL

PRAISE FOR *HOPES FOR SCHOOL*

"As someone deeply invested in the future of education, I found this book both eye-opening and inspiring. *Hopes for School* is a powerful call to action. It challenges educators to rethink their practices, to listen to their students, and to create learning environments that are both engaging and empowering. It urges teachers to foster an environment where students can make mistakes, where they are encouraged to engage with their curiosity, and where they can choose how they want to demonstrate their learning. The book's emphasis on authentic learning with real-world applications made me excited about how these ideas can transform education for the better. I am excited about the potential this book has to inspire change and make education a more positive and enriching experience for all students."

—**Luis Fernando Pertuz Escribano,** data analysis and management, Marymount School, Colombia, Google Innovator and Trainer

"*Hopes for School* is powerfully written, honest, and real. Everything you would hope for in a professional book in education: stories that resonate, applicable strategies and takeaways, countless opportunities to reflect on our own practices, examples from educators—AND the honest lived experiences of our students!"

—**Carly Spina,** multilingual education specialist, Illinois Resource Center

"Captivating. Insightful. Empowering. Through the lens of learners of all ages, this solution-oriented book beautifully weaves together compelling stories of challenges and successes. Kids truly are the most precious, abundant, and underutilized resource in our learning communities, and this book unlocks the power of being learner-centered through connections, inquiry, and innovation. With *Hopes for School*, we can reflect on our current practices, prioritize meaningful shifts, and spark courageous conversations. An essential read for anyone ready to make a difference in our schools!"

—**Lainie Rowell,** bestselling author, award-winning educator, and international keynote speaker

"*Hopes for School* is a unique collaboration that brings the authentic voice of the student to the forefront of educational discourse. Karen Phan's candid reflections on her school experiences, paired with Jennifer Casa-Todd's insightful educational context and practical strategies, create a powerful dialogue that is both engaging and enlightening. This book offers invaluable perspectives for educators seeking to truly understand and improve the student experience. It's a must-read for anyone committed to fostering a more empathetic and effective learning environment."

—**Mandy Froehlich,** educator, author, and mental health advocate

"This book is for any educator who wants to disrupt the status quo and reinvent what school can be. Boldly written, rooted in research, and filled with practical strategies, this book is for the dreamers who are doers. It's for those of us who are crazy enough to believe that maybe we can change the world—maybe by changing the way we do school."

—**Meghan Lawson,** author, speaker, and district leader

KAREN PHAN & JENNIFER CASA-TODD

HOPES FOR SCHOOL

A STUDENT'S EXPERIENCE
AND IDEAS FOR
EDUCATIONAL TRANSFORMATION

Hopes for School: A Student's Experience and Ideas for Educational Transformation
© 2025 Karen Phan with Jennifer Casa-Todd

All rights reserved. No part of this publication may be reproduced in any form or by any electronic or mechanical means, including information storage and retrieval systems, without permission in writing by the publisher, except by a reviewer who may quote brief passages in a review. For information regarding permission, contact the publisher at books@impressbooks.org.

> This book is available at special discounts when purchased in quantity for educational purposes or for use as premiums, promotions, or fundraisers. For inquiries and details, contact the publisher at books@impressbooks.org.

Published by IMPress, a division of Dave Burgess Consulting, Inc.
IMPressbooks.org
DaveBurgessConsulting.com
Vancouver, WA

Library of Congress Control Number: 2025934290
Paperback ISBN: 978-1-948334-79-2
Ebook ISBN: 978-1-948334-80-8

Cover and interior design by Liz Schreiter
Edited and produced by Reading List Editorial
ReadingListEditorial.com

CONTENTS

Foreword 1
Introduction 4
Chapter 1: Mistakes 17
Chapter 2: Grades 41
Chapter 3: Connections 65
Chapter 4: Homework 91
Chapter 5: Make School More Practical 111
Chapter 6: Student Voice, Choice, and Agency 140
Concluding Thoughts 166

Endnotes 170
Acknowledgments 180
About the Authors 182
More from IMPress 184

FOREWORD

I remember the epiphany well—the look on their faces, a mix of ennui, exhaustion, exasperation. That class of seniors (it was the first time I had taught that level in years, back when I was student teaching) staring back at me, beat. We had read through *Beowulf*, *Sir Gawain and the Green Knight*, *Macbeth*. I dutifully doled out worksheets, carefully crafted questions to help them understand these ancient texts. I quizzed them, tested them, to ensure they remembered what was important to remember: diction, tone, theme, those universal truths that have stood true for hundreds—thousands!—of years.

I don't remember who said it, or what piece of classwork or homework the student was referring to, but their question matched their bleary-eyed look, and it rattled me.

"Can you just tell me what to do to get an A on this?"

I knew I had to do something different. The status quo wasn't engaging students, and it wasn't preparing them for much more than taking class-based multiple choice or standardized tests. And for all the talk of gearing students up for college AND a career, relying solely on such tests weren't going to cut it.

One of my first pedagogical shifts was to give my students permission to question the whys and hows of their education. If we're going to saddle them with tens of thousands of dollars (or more!) of student debt, they should know why they're sitting in our classrooms waiting to be netted up by all those big, fancy colleges they dream of attending. So before my students open up *The Catcher in the Rye*, I lead them through the Question Formulation Technique, a question-brainstorming session in which they crank out a list of questions based on this statement: *school is the best place to learn.* They pare down their list of questions to just a couple and then explore that question as they read Salinger, Prose, Emerson, Baldwin. Students then publish their explorations on the web.

The book that you hold in your hands began in one such brainstorm. It began as one question by Karen Phan, a curious, witty sixteen-year-old student. The title of her exploration? "I'm a Loser Because of School."

As you will soon discover for yourself, Karen is definitely *not* a loser. But as a reporter for our school newspaper, Karen often wielded hyperbole to catch readers' attention in her opinion pieces, and as her adviser, I found myself defending her exaggerations when they rubbed my colleagues the wrong way. But Karen was always right in some way. Karen could cut through to truth.

Through Karen's reading, research, and writing about how school works and its effect on her and other students, she had discovered what sculptor Claes Oldenburg calls a "kernel of infinite expansion." I read about Oldenburg's "kernel" in Geoffrey Sirc's *English Composition as a Happening*, which suggests we teach "writing as growing, changing, maybe even culturally transforming."

My goal for all my students is that they will find something they love to write about, something that they can't help writing about for years to come, a "kernel" they can expand on indefinitely. Sirc's book, a three-hundred-page riff on Charles Deemer's 1967 essay of the same name, supercharged my classroom practice. In the chapter titled "The American Action Writers," Sirc argues Jackson Pollock "became a real [artist] only when he began to follow his heart: discovering he had a vision and voice worth sharing."

In this book, Karen follows her heart. She *loves* to learn, and she has a vision for how schools and teachers can help students recapture this love. And I think you'll agree with me that Karen's voice is one worth sharing, as are the other voices in this book. I hope as teachers try out Karen's and Jen's suggestions along with those of other students and teachers, we can "culturally transform" our classrooms and campuses to prioritize learning over schooling.

How could we not when we transform our classrooms into places of "joyful struggle" using the Question Matrix Lindsay Werner describes in chapter 1? How could we not prioritize learning over grading when we provide students with feedback first and a grade second, as Jen suggests in chapter 2? Or if we dedicate time to knowing our students' names, faces, and stories like Jason Trinh and Mary Hemphill encourage us to do in chapter 3, how could our students' achievement not increase as we transform our classrooms into *communities* of learners?

Trinh reminds teachers "we sometimes rely on our versions of who we think our students are." Sirc wonders about the problem this way: "Are our students searching for a way to make the world see the world their way, or, rather, do we insist they be made to [see] the world the way we think it's supposed to be seen?" I hope you'll help your students make the world see things their way. How else can we help them build the world they'll be living in after we're gone?

Read this book. Try out just one or two of the myriad strategies it proposes. See school the way Karen sees it, which will help you see your classroom the way your students see it. Your students will notice, and, together, you'll be transformed.

—Sean Ziebarth

INTRODUCTION

FROM THE STUDENT'S DESK: KAREN

When I was seven or eight, I had to do a three-month research project about dinosaurs for school. There were instructions and a simple rubric, but grades don't mean anything to second and third graders, so I didn't care. I didn't even know what a rubric was supposed to be. I was just excited. I loved projects because I was a creative and crafty kid, and I was fascinated by the La Brea Tar Pits, which we had recently read about. I dove into this project headfirst, driven purely by my curiosity. I wanted to go beyond what we'd learned in class, but no one in my household was fluent in English, so I had to figure things out for myself. Article after article, YouTube video after YouTube video, I got lost in the rabbit hole as I spent hours researching dinosaurs. And I didn't want to find a way out of that rabbit hole, either. All those *Dinosaur Train* episodes convinced me I could become the world's youngest paleontologist. I ended up getting a 4 on the project (the equivalent of an A), but as a kid, you don't care about that stuff. I was more content with all the knowledge I had gained about dinosaurs. It was never about the grade—whatever that even was—but about learning (and making the prettiest trifold poster).

At that time, school was about learning, and it was my favorite place. It stayed that way until we started having fewer opportunities to be in charge of our own learning and to be creative. Then, school and learning started to diverge. That was in the fifth grade. I walked on this fuzzy line between learning and schooling, between answering my own questions and answering the questions on a complex rubric for my essay about Noah Webster. No offense to anyone who is a fan of "the father of American scholarship and education," but I did not choose to write about him nor did I enjoy writing about him.

I didn't get a perfect grade on that essay. It made me feel terrible. I liked writing, but being perfect and getting good grades started mattering so much more. Bad grade equaled bad student and bad writer. As a college student now, I realize that that essay was the blossoming of my dislike for school because of how perfect the rubric demanded everything be. The more I wrote, the more unconfident I became—I questioned every word I put down. Did my writing match the expectations detailed in the rubric? At the end of writing this essay, I was fully baptized, soaked in a pool of hatred for school and my own writing. All I wanted was to be perfect, which meant conforming to the rigid expectations laid before me and following the step-by-step formula for success that others had created. There was no more doing things for my genuine interests. No more freedom. No more creativity. No more learning.

So I spent fifth, sixth, seventh, eighth, ninth, tenth, eleventh, and twelfth grade trying to be perfect. I've spent a whole seven years since my Noah Webster essay doing a whole lot of school and becoming good at it, but, if I'm honest, I don't think I've done a whole lot of learning in school. The word "school" doesn't make me think of engagement, lightbulbs, and collaboration. Instead, all that comes to mind are two-part tests, falling asleep at 4:00 a.m., mental breakdowns, and soggy school lunches. Getting As, what I could put on my college application, and my almost innate desire to satisfy adults drove me much more than my curiosity in high school. What once was my favorite place on earth became one of my least favorite places on earth, often feeling monotonous and dull.

That's the opposite of what learning is to me. Spontaneous. Intuitive. Unpredictable. Learning is fun, free, and all about you.

Learning is creating something meaningful and unique to you, not just consuming and regurgitating. Learning is forever and self-driven.

The problem is that many students have been trained to think that schooling is learning. Stellar stats, for example, do not equate to being intelligent and talented, yet many school districts define students with numbers. So naturally, the first word that comes to mind when describing someone who scored 35 on the ACT is "smart." I see teens on TikTok subtly flex their 4.5 GPA with hundreds of comments raving about how "smart" they are, when the fact is that these students are not more intelligent than their peers who have a 3.2 GPA. I don't intend to discredit the hard work of 4.5 GPA students, but I graduated from high school with a 4.4 GPA and I would not say that I am more knowledgeable and talented than someone who has a 3.2 GPA. Maybe that person is doing bigger and better things outside of school. Maybe they're dedicated to pursuing their passion and carving their own path to success. Or school just isn't for them, and they thrive outside of an academic environment. I can only sincerely say that I am better at doing what I'm told to do, taking tests, and complying with the school system.

I made a student survey to brainstorm ideas for this book. One of the questions was "Complete the sentence: The purpose of school is…"

> *to make students into workers.*
> *to get good grades and graduate.*
> *to prepare us for the future.*
> *to provide [a] social and life experience for as many people as possible.*
> *to develop young adults by giving them education, social skills, and a purpose to contribute to society.*
> *to get a better chance of getting a job.*
> *to find what you're interested in and make friends.*
> *to learn.*

That last response is not entirely true for many students. We spend years of our lives being trained by this system to be employable and compliant and are told over and over again that we go to school to "learn."

But if the purpose of school is to learn, the students who responded to my survey wouldn't have told me that they're afraid to make mistakes, which is an integral part of learning, and that they always put their grades first. If the purpose of school is to learn, students wouldn't be forced to conform to the same standards and be deemed failures when they step out of line. If the purpose of school is to learn, taking risks would be more beneficial than detrimental. If the purpose of school is to learn, self-direction and personalization of education would exist to a greater extent than it does now.

The fact is that we're here to school, and all the schooling we've done may have actually messed up our understanding of learning, leading to the conflation of "school" and "learning."

This shouldn't be much of a surprise. The American education system gets an A+ for killing students' creativity. Here, education is a tool to condition, not to expand one's mind. Sir Ken Robinson, a British author and adviser on education, said during his famous 2006 TED Talk "Do Schools Kill Creativity?" that "many highly talented, brilliant, creative people think they're not, because the thing they were good at at school wasn't valued, or was actually stigmatized" due to public education being "a protracted process of university entrance."[1] I interpreted his talk as meaning that schooling institutions manufacture the typical route to "success" as going to school, getting good grades, going to college, and then getting a job with that degree you got. It's generic, boring, pressuring, and limiting, but as much as I and the millions of other American students out there may dislike school, there's no way for us to scream anarchy and overthrow the system.

We still need to get a job and make a living. Everything important that we work hard for—our grades, GPAs, and class rank—boils down to getting into college so we can live a comfortable life and have value in American society. With college admissions becoming more competitive each year, students will do *anything* to stay at the front of the race. From purchasing the AP United States History exams on Course Hero and memorizing the answers the night before the test to volunteering only because we need service hours, unhappy and stressed-out students will do anything and everything to stay in the front of the pack. The sleepless nights and cheating can get extreme, but school continues to get harder and harder, leaving students with few options to challenge the education system without jeopardizing their prospects for success in the world of employment and status that school is built for. It's better—safer—to *not* pick yourself. It's better to learn how to succeed in the system and work through it to graduate in the top 10 percent of your class than potentially risk your future.

This is a reality I'm used to because I thrive in school and am surrounded by people who also thrive in school. The white graduation gown that I wore, given to students with cumulative GPAs of 4.0 and greater, is a fleeting testament to our success in making the fewest mistakes possible. I sit in class with my head empty, no thoughts, because I'm used to consuming all the material and then forgetting it after the test. I have no intention of putting my spin on things. Sometimes I feel as though I have no passion and ambition because I try to be good at everything and have no time or energy to explore what interests me. I am so used to schooling and am so good at it that I'm uncomfortable when I imagine what school would be like if it inspired rather than conditioned students.

So when my eleventh-grade English teacher, Sean Ziebarth, allowed my class to self-direct our learning through a Question Exploration, wherein we ask our own questions prior to reading a book and discover the answers to them, I was initially confused, scared, and angry. "What do I have to do to get an A?" "Why can't you just give me a detailed rubric?" "Why do I have to figure this out by myself?" "Why do I have to think for myself?" "Do my ideas have meaning and relevance?" "Am I capable of having my own ideas?" (For the record, Mr. Ziebarth did give us a simple rubric.) The assignment pissed me off because I had no idea where to begin—to the point that I procrastinated and did the entire thing the week it was due even though we had over a month to work on it. When I worked on the Question Exploration, I felt this odd sense of familiarity as I ended up with over fifteen tabs open on my screen, but why?

I felt like I was in elementary school again, obsessively reading about dinosaurs and decorating my trifold poster for hours. This time, I was obsessively reading about education and trying to answer "Why does school make me a loser?" for hours. I was discovering the answer to *my question* and creating a blog post unique and meaningful to me. There was a rubric, but I didn't care about it anymore because it was an assignment I learned I was passionate about. At that moment, school wasn't about the grade. It was, for the first time in years, about learning.

I finished my Question Exploration, which I called "I'm a Loser Because of School," with a strong sense of the loserness instilled. Although I'm extremely proud of my identity as a student and don't take any part of my education for granted, I also came to have a clearer understanding of why, exactly, I don't consider school to be a place of learning.

It might be strange to think that when you consider that for many students, school provides a level playing field. School is where there are teachers to help guide you and books to read from, where there are printers and tutors and countless other resources to assist students. But despite the plethora of resources and the passion of teachers who propel students forward, learners are ill-directed because the emphasis of school is on memorizing as much information as possible, getting tested on it, and then passing. It's not about learning and enriching the mind.

My criticism of schooling isn't to say that school is an inherently bad place to be. Some parts of school are good. Take what we learned from the COVID-19 pandemic. With schools across the United States shuttered, the social and in-person interactions between students and teachers were reduced to our faces being displayed as tiny stamps on a screen during video conferences. Social interaction is good, and for many adults and students, school provides a fun environment, whether in table groups or at lunch. Taking away those live interactions in class, and even those lunches together in the quad where seagulls like to poop out of nowhere, made me miss my friends and value school. On a larger scale, it made clear to school leaders, educators, students, and parents that the basis of teaching comes down to relationships and interactions between teachers and students.

But distance learning during the COVID-19 pandemic also showed us that when you take away the social aspect of school, school is boring. The only thing students do is sit in their seats and consume information from 8:00 a.m. to 2:00 p.m. day after day.

Learning includes the consumption of information, but it's never bounded consumption. Learning is a constant and authentic creation of what you believe is important and want to know. Unfortunately, we students are used to answering other people's questions and being led by educators instead of asking our own questions and cocreating or self-directing our learning.

So on the off chance that students, especially at the older grade levels, *do* have a say in their education, they freak out. I found out that so many of my peers didn't like doing the Question Exploration, a learner-driven assignment. They had the same complaints and frustrations as I did when I started. It was too hard to come up with an original idea that matters to us. We just wanted to know what we had to do to get an A. But while I finished it absolutely in love and motivated to continue self-directing my learning whenever I could, my friends still did not see the value in the Question Exploration.

The lasting reaction to the Question Exploration from my peers still bothers me. It was fun and liberating. We were free to do whatever we wanted, so how could it have been a bad thing?

Later on, I realized it was overwhelming for some students because it's been ages since we could self-direct our learning. Schooling is like riding a bike with training wheels and someone holding on to you the whole time. Learning is taking away those training wheels and that person letting go, and then falling and getting back up over and over until you've figured out all the little tricks. We'd been using training wheels since our first day of school, so Mr. Ziebarth taking those away from us as high school juniors inevitably left us crashing into walls. Mr. Ziebarth created a space for us to have the free will and ingenuity to be in charge of our education and pursue what matters to us, but so many students do not know what self-directed learning is because they haven't experienced it so long in school, and therefore they do not value these rare opportunities.

When I reflect on my schooling, I'm sad. Sad that school stifled my creativity. Sad that I felt like I lost a piece of my brain every day at school. Sad that the school system conditioned free will and ingenuity out of me. While conducting research for this book, I was heartened to learn that there are student-centered schools in North America that challenge traditional K–12 educational practices. I also heard from students with more positive experiences with school than I had. They shared that they enjoy school and believe it's the best place for them to learn. And I came across so many teachers on social media who've spoken out against the bad parts of schooling and shared their classroom practices that empower students to take charge of their education.

The problem is that we keep hearing school administrators and district leaders talk about the "relevant stakeholders" involved, but I wonder how often and effectively they consult student opinions. Every single member of our society has a stake in the well-being of our youth, but students are arguably the most important stakeholders because it's *our education*. The education system shouldn't exist solely to prepare us to be moldable employees, but to empower us to be creative, happy, and expressive individuals who are knowledgeable and possess valuable and practical skills, and who will propel society forward with our unique talents. These "relevant stakeholders" are supposed to include students, but I remember having no say in my high school district (which functions as a bureaucracy), nor do millions of other students. If there are opportunities to get involved in the decision-making process, the majority of students either aren't aware or they're apathetic because they've been trained to believe that their ideas and uniqueness bring nothing meaningful to the table.

I want this to change. I want students to truly be at the center of their education, but we don't even have a say in what our daily lessons could look like. Us spearheading a movement to reform the education system seems next to impossible. Our voices—student voices—are important yet are not amplified enough. Although there are schools and teachers who are doing it right by valuing students and letting us take the lead in our learning, it's undeniable that our current education and pedagogy are still largely teacher-centered, content-driven, and outdated. Students can speak out all we want, but we remain trapped in an unapologetic system that gatekeeps our futures and careers. Reforming school is a sustained and collaborative effort from students, parents, teachers, administrators, and legislators. But change on a large scale is also slow and difficult, and school being the monolith it is doesn't make this task any easier.

I'm writing from a position of privilege: I grew up in a community that highly values education, received excellent public education, and had no obligations that interfered with my schooling. I attribute so much of my success as a young adult to school. School did a lot of good for me, and I think this good could be made better available to more people. My hope for this book is to change the narrative for other students who may be experiencing school the same way I have and to suggest more student-centered, easy-to-implement strategies that teachers can incorporate into their classrooms at any level. I want to shed light on some problems students face so I can showcase the perspectives of students, which are too often missing from these stakeholder meetings. I want to encourage schools to have conversations with students about the unique challenges they face that I can't speak to. It's time to invite students to the table because we deserve to have a voice in what our future should look like.

FROM THE TEACHER'S DESK: JENNIFER

I met Karen through George Couros, who told me about Karen's book idea. I jumped at the chance to work with a student who was writing a book based on what she was hoping to see change in education. As the cofounder of the Global Student Chat and a self-proclaimed amplifier of student voices, I inherently feel like listening to students and their experiences can help us better our craft and make education itself better as well. Several years ago, the Ontario government invited a student task force to give feedback on what they valued in their education, and their motto was "Nothing about us, without us." I loved this and have made it a point to teach and lead by this stance. (Couros specifically references his own hopes for school in *The Innovator's Mindset Podcast*, which is what inspired the title for this book.[2])

HOPES FOR SCHOOL
THE INNOVATOR'S MINDSET PODCAST

Learners will feel welcome and valued in school and the classrooms.

We will start by focusing on the strengths and passions of each learner.

Learners will feel that their contributions are necessary to the success of the class and school as a whole.

If I am being honest with you and myself, coauthoring a book with a student who is a brilliant writer and an A student who actually admits to hating school has been at times very challenging because it is really hard to read her words without getting defensive. I told myself a few times as I read her perspective that, as a student, she has no idea of the pressures on us to do more with less and to be at the whim of governments who cut funds or implement programs that may not be best for kids. I wanted to reach out to her to say that she doesn't realize the extent to which we have students in front of us whose learning needs are so different that it feels like an impossible task to meet all of them. Karen knows of her own parental pressures but doesn't realize the extent to which parents and families are intricately related to our ability to teach the students in our care. And sometimes I found myself wondering if Karen is just a disgruntled teen who is blaming school rather than taking responsibility for her own learning. I rationalized that this is just the perspective of one student and that the experiences shared here may not be shared by the majority of my students. Are they? And also, isn't being ornery the very foundation of adolescence? I know why I had this reaction: at times her words are hard to read and not take personally.

As Karen shared the impact school has had on her and her well-being, I found myself both heartbroken and reflective of my own practices and those within my school. Karen's perspective, along with the "What Works for Me" segments in this book, helped me to realize that I need to hear what she has to say; we all do. Karen isn't a disgruntled teen writing a book to complain about education: she is a young woman with a desire to share her experiences so her younger sister and others experience school differently. As I read and reflected on her words, I was inspired to talk to my students and my colleagues about what I was reading, to tweak what I was already doing or take a risk to try something new. Today, Karen is an accomplished young woman who is successful in spite of her experiences. Even so, all of our students deserve to look back on their time at school and recall positive, student-centered learning experiences.

Although the bulk of this book is written by Karen, the "From the Teacher's Desk" segments provide a vehicle for me to reflect on what Karen is sharing as it applies to my own practice and highlight some of the ideas that have been successful for me. I have been teaching a long time, and with that comes a natural tendency to reflect on the practices of my younger self. Much of what I share is either research based or action-research based in that they are practices that have been successful in my teaching and co-teaching. I've never taught at a fancy school; My experiences are based in public education in Ontario, Canada. I am bound by government curriculum restrictions and standardized tests, as well as the constraints of district and union policies. When I read Karen's experiences, even though she went to school thousands of miles away from me, I recognized the practices that prevented her from being fully engaged in school—perhaps too much so.

Because I am blessed to be connected to an international community of educators online, I also recognized that many educators have shifted their teaching practices to embrace more innovative approaches. There are a plethora of professional learning books out there that have helped teachers along the way. It was important for me to bring in other voices and practical ideas and strategies around Karen's themes through "Idea Spotlights." These are by no means exhaustive. In fact, it is our hope that when you read this book, if you have an Idea Spotlight to share, you will do so on our collaborative Padlet found at jcasatodd.com or by using the hashtag #HopesForSchool on your favorite social media platform.

Coauthoring this book has been soul nourishing because I got to know Karen personally and realize that her hopes for this book are to make education better. Just as I have learned from reading about Karen's experiences, so, too, do I hope that her reflections and ideas resonate with you, whether you are reading this book alone or as a book study with a group of educators, and whether you are a first-year or veteran teacher. It is our hope that this book might reinforce the great work you are already doing, or that it might inspire you to select one thing you would like to prioritize and tweak in your own practice. We hope that the discussion questions inspire courageous conversations among staff, administration, and even district leaders.

CHAPTER 1
MISTAKES

> "There's a problem with trying to understand every mistake you've made... you can't... And trying to robs you of your life, your plans, your future. Plus, you can't really learn from your mistakes if you stop moving forward."
>
> — GREY'S ANATOMY

FROM THE STUDENT'S DESK: KAREN

I'm a college student, and sometimes I'm stuck in middle school. I still remember the mistakes I made in seventh grade on a pre-algebra perimeter and area quiz. That was over five years ago. One of the questions was to find the area of a semicircle, and I forgot to divide the area of the circle in half. Another asked if a rectangular object could fit into a circular rug. Instead of using the diameter to find the circumference of the circle, I used the radius.

I also remember that I spelled "sweater" wrong on a mini-narrative in second grade, and that I didn't know what eight times seven was during a math bee in third grade, and that I conjugated "jugar" when it was supposed to be in its infinitive form on a Spanish test, and—you get the point. I remember them all. Mistakes, especially the ones in school, are all I think about for days and days; I randomly remember them years later and roll around in bed in frustration at 4:00 a.m. They stay with me forever. I never get over my mistakes. Ever.

Luckily, I usually don't make the same mistakes again; I got 100 percent on the second pre-algebra quiz and test for that same chapter I initially did poorly on. But I become a more fearful student each day. Inside the classroom, I chased perfection (until senioritis kicked in when I was a high school senior and things went downhill), and coping with mistakes isn't something I'm good at. I know mistakes are valuable, especially when they lead to learning, and I'm open to making them outside the classroom. But inside the classroom, in American education, I ignore Meredith Grey's words and avoid making mistakes at all costs.

My attitude toward mistakes hasn't always been like this. Elementary me never saw mistakes as a bad thing. I spelled "sweater" wrong in my mini-narrative, but I don't recall feeling sad or frustrated about it because I was happy that my teacher enjoyed my story as a whole. At the time, I didn't view mistakes as imperfections to agonize over. I thought they were normal things that happened all the time, so I just moved on—and that's what mistakes really are. But by the time I got to middle school, my tolerance for mistakes weakened in the face of one-size-fits-all learning, weekly tests, and the pressure to achieve a 4.0 GPA.

AMERICAN EDUCATION ISN'T BUILT FOR MISTAKES

In my experience, school minimizes mistakes from the start, and a lot of things in American education are predetermined. Unknown and distant governing bodies create schedules, curricula, and sets of standards that teachers need to teach the same way and that students need to master the same way. There's a certain way you need to solve this math problem in order to get full points on a test. There's a certain structure you need to follow and a formal tone you always need to have in order to get full points on your essays.

Standardizing almost everything means that, on one hand, there's some uniformity in education—all students build a similar foundation of discipline and skills and a reservoir of knowledge by the time they leave their schooling institutions. On the other hand, spending twelve-plus years in a rigid education system that has outlined every step of the way for us to be "good students" and told us what we need to know and how we need to know it has created students who have trouble handling when someone isn't holding their hand at all times.

The beauty of learning is that it's an *imperfect* and spontaneous process, but the last time learning in school was truly like that for me was in preschool and elementary school. Although standardization, report cards, and assessments exist in these early years of education, no one really cares about them. My teachers, parents, peers, and I never dwelled on these. This part of my education was about building a foundation so once I entered middle school, I could read books, write paragraphs, do basic algebra, use technology, and socialize, among other things that were all more important than being perfect.

As I got older, I found that standardization became a more prominent part of school. There was a sense of urgency to get through material quickly and efficiently. I had to get things right on the first try because one bad score would tank my overall grade even if I got ten good scores. School defined the "right" and "wrong" way to go about solving problems, and anything different was considered a mistake. I became less creative in school and stopped questioning my environment because I found there were few opportunities for me to do things my way without being academically punished. I felt stuck.

Ironically, this focus on how things are "supposed to be done" runs counter to the "growth mindset" teachers often encourage us to have. Instead, anti-mistake culture stifles growth mindset.

And not only can allowing for mistakes promote students' individual creativity and unique point of view; mistakes can actually improve learning outcomes. In her 2017 article "Learning from Errors," Dr. Janet Metcalfe dissects the anti-mistake mentality that is so prevalent in American education and proposes that "error avoidance" and "errorless learning" might be "a counterproductive strategy, at least for neurologically typical students."[1]

Making mistakes and *addressing them* benefits learning because it encourages students to reflect on what went wrong. Having conversations about mistakes and articulating thought processes around them with teachers and peers helps students understand their mistakes and how they might approach future problems differently. Metcalfe notes in her paper that providing "corrective feedback" and fostering an environment that is tolerant of and even encourages mistakes benefits both teachers and students because students will be more engaged and eager to explore. The error-avoidance mentality and error-avoidance approaches in American education are not needed when we learn to emphasize giving, receiving, and utilizing feedback in school. In classrooms that embrace making errors and allow students to learn from them, I'd expect to see many students actually take on a growth mindset because mistakes wouldn't bring about fear and embarrassment. Instead, they'd be a valuable step in the learning process.

As Robert B. Reich wrote in his op-ed "One Education Does Not Fit All" in 2000, students who don't conform to the mold the education system created are viewed as "uneducable."[2] More than twenty years later, his words still ring true. School tells students who get bad grades or can't keep up with the pace of their classrooms that they're stupid, hopeless, lost causes, problem children, and lacking potential. They're mistakes.[3] If we don't want students to feel this way in an environment that's for learning and socialization, then we need to change how we view and treat mistakes in school.

WHAT WORKS FOR ME

In our current anti-mistake education culture, mistakes may at first feel isolated, like little hiccups along the road to learning. But as those mistakes begin to add up, students may begin to feel like *they* are the real mistakes.

That's what happened to me in my first semester of AP Calculus BC. Math isn't one of my strong subjects, but I took this class anyway because I felt obligated to after taking years of accelerated math classes. Calculus was much more difficult than I expected. I had a C in the class one month into school and got Fs on quizzes. I couldn't withdraw from the class because the withdrawal deadline had passed. I was so stressed out that I started having nightmares about calculus—I had one about derivatives the night before my derivatives test. It felt like the world was ending. I felt like the dumbest student on earth and that I had no place in this course.

This feeling was especially crushing because outside of this class I did everything else right to be a model student. I graduated from high school with a cumulative 4.4 GPA. I took AP classes, participated in school clubs, and volunteered. I think about what school wants me to know, when school wants me to know it, and how school wants me to know it. I'm good at following directions. I've settled into the system, even now in college. And I'm not the only one who fits into the cookie cutter. I am the same as every other good student in the nation.

Erica Goldson, a valedictorian, spoke out against schooling in 2010 in her graduation speech, talking about how this one-size-fits-all model makes students feel like mistakes: "Between these cinder block walls, we are all expected to be the same. We are trained to ace every standardized test, and those who deviate and see light through a different lens are worthless to the scheme of public education, and therefore viewed with contempt."[4]

I don't think schooling has changed much since Goldson's time because my friend Eric, a student from Huntington Beach, California, has a similar sentiment to Goldson. He says the school system takes away from our ability to grow, learn, create, and question because "everything is presented in only one manner."

So what are some more effective strategies that teachers might use to save us from the nightmares and self-doubt—to create a safe space for mistakes?

1. GIVE STUDENTS SECOND CHANCES.

When my sister was in first grade, one of the things I found so fascinating about her class was how she had the opportunity to redo her homework. Using educational apps such as Seesaw and IXL, my sister was given multiple, immediate opportunities to try again when she got a question wrong. Learning from mistakes was built into the structure of learning itself.

In my experience, that fell away by middle and high school. The opportunities to redo my work were limited to rare test corrections. Older students may not need to redo every single assignment to figure out what they got wrong, but especially for larger assignments that carry the bulk of the grade, students should have ample opportunity for revision. Giving students second chances can include allowing them to do test corrections, redo assignments that they scored a C or below on, and revise their essays for a higher grade. Students will be less fearful of mistakes if they know they're on a learning journey with second chances built in.

Something I started to do in college to make revision more meaningful to me was set goals with my instructor—my first college humanities professor—at the beginning of our essays. I set these goals based on feedback he gave me on my last paper, and during our one-on-one meetings, he gave me advice on how I could meet these goals. I also bring these goals and any concerns I have to my university's writing center to get help from peer tutors. It's an effective practice for me because I know what I want to achieve, and my professor also knows what parts of my essay I'd like him to help me with. I did something similar when I was the editor in chief of my high school newspaper by encouraging writers to leave a comment at the top of their articles to let their editors know what they specifically wanted feedback on. This made the editing process more mindful for both writers and editors, so I can imagine it would be a useful practice in the classroom, too.

But in the meantime, there are a few ways to work around issues regarding a lack of time. To potentially lighten the revision and regrading workload for teachers, we can do more peer reviewing.[5] It's a great way to get students involved in their learning by giving each other feedback instead of depending on just one teacher for feedback. I wrote about this in a post for my school newspaper called "Students Benefit More from Peer Reviewing than They Think They Do."[6] I love doing peer reviewing with a group of three to four students because it allows me to receive feedback from multiple perspectives and learn how my classmates think.

Some students have trouble with peer reviewing because they don't know where to start. Teachers can help start the peer revision process by critiquing some student work (with permission, of course) with the class so students know what to look for and what the expectations are, and how to approach giving and receiving feedback. In one of my English classes, we did peer reviewing through the "glow and grow" method by identifying specific parts of the work that were excellent and then parts that could be improved. If I wanted to give someone a glow comment, I'd say something along the lines of "The part that interests me most about your writing is..." To give a grow comment, I'd say, "Can you share more details about . . ."

2. ENCOURAGE STUDENTS TO "FAIL FORWARD."

Author and leadership coach Dr. Margie Warrell wrote that schools need to normalize failure and encourage students to "fail forward." Failing forward teaches students to view each mistake as a part of the learning process rather than a roadblock. Failing forward encourages constructive feedback, reflection, and opportunities to try again and self-improve, in place of academic punishments. Getting rid of grades once and for all will take a while (if it'll ever actually happen), so here's a method that's easier to incorporate: Failure Week.

According to Warrell, Failure Week is when teachers celebrate failure for a week by sharing their mistakes and how they've learned from them. All schools can implement Failure Week, and teachers can even hold failure sessions on a regular basis. During each session, students reflect by writing or talking about a mistake they recently made and how they learned from that mistake. Such reflections also show students how valuable failing is, which teaches them to bounce back rather than lie in bed and vow to never do whatever they failed in again. It teaches them that they learn more from their mistakes and trying again than their continuous success.

Encouraging students to share their failures creates a "culture of courage" as well.[7] Californian student Lylyan wrote in an opinion article that "the fear of being wrong is evident in participation. Very few students participate and answer questions in class because speaking up in class is a struggle for many students. Many, including myself, also do not participate because we fear answering the question wrong and humiliating ourselves in front of more than thirty of our peers."[8] Imagine—if that fear disappeared, how many students would be leaping to participate?

The idea of Failure Week doesn't have to be a one-time thing, either. It might be fun to do an activity to embrace mistakes on a weekly basis or incorporate failure into daily lessons and overall classroom culture. The syllabus for an introductory programming class I took in college states the following: "You WILL make a lot of mistakes as you first learn to code. We will ALL make mistakes when programming. It's a good thing!! We encourage you to make LOTS of them, & to LEARN from them."

My professor wasn't joking. I made mistakes every single day while learning to code, but I didn't feel bad about them because she made it clear that making these mistakes and understanding them is how we would become better programmers. During every lecture, we wrote and dissected programs together, proposed modifications to our code, and saw why our code would or wouldn't work. The e-book we used to complete our programming labs always gave us instant feedback when there was an issue with our submission and allowed us to resubmit as many times as we needed to get the problems correct. Programming requires precision and accuracy, but it also has a fun and experimental side. At the end of the day, the goal is to figure out the best way to solve a problem, so there are lots of things you'll be testing out until you get it right. Taking this programming class made me more comfortable with making mistakes because I know they're a part of learning, building a foundation, and they can help me become a better programmer.

We need more Failure Week concepts and mistakes in school because as students come to understand that failure is OK, we'll slowly stop being afraid. We'll take baby steps, from raising our hands in class to questioning a lesson to choosing a hard assignment. We'll fail, but we'll get up and work hard because we know mistakes have a place in learning.[9]

STUDENT SPOTLIGHT

Students learn better when they feel safe and valued. My teacher has created a positive and inclusive classroom environment by promoting mutual respect, empathy, and understanding. This approach encouraged students to participate and share their ideas. Also, meaningful feedback helped the students to know how they are progressing and where they need to improve. The regular feedback that is specific, constructive, and actionable helps students to learn from their mistakes and make progress toward their goals. My teacher encouraged collaboration by providing opportunities to us to work together on projects and activities. It helped students to develop their social skills and learn from one another.

NAMYA JOSHI, ELEVENTH GRADE, INDIA

FROM THE TEACHER'S DESK: JENNIFER

At first I was shocked that an honors student, committed to academic success, was sharing her intense fear of making mistakes. And yet, it makes complete sense that a student like Karen, who gets good grades, would suffer from perfectionism. Reading about her experiences made me think of my students for whom school did not come easily or who would rather come across as a class clown or completely uncaring than face school failure after school failure. Did I serve those students well? Am I aware of the extent to which a child or adolescent would want to save face above all else?

When I think about the red pen I used to "correct mistakes" and then read Karen's perspective here, I wish I could go back and apologize to every student I ever taught in my early years of teaching. I know I didn't recognize how my students might be internalizing my corrections. I remember having a Wall of Shame whereby students were encouraged to bring in photos of misspelled menus or signs so we could post them. It didn't occur to me how students would then feel terrified of their own mistakes. Talk about a teacher-fail. When you know better, you do better, and so I switched from red to purple pen and scrapped the Wall of Shame. The following are a few of the practices that allowed my students to see failures and mistakes as a part of the learning process or that allowed students of varying abilities to demonstrate their learning in a way that supported their own strengths.

DIFFERENTIATED PRODUCTS

This line from Karen's point of view was really hard to read: "School tells students who get bad grades or can't keep up with the pace of their classrooms that they're stupid, hopeless, lost causes, problem children, and lacking potential. They're mistakes." No teacher ever intends for this outcome, and this statement made me reflect on my practice and wonder if my own students who weren't doing well in my course felt this way. For a long time (longer than I wish), I focused on my curriculum: content before kids, so to speak. Later I began to wonder if some of my students weren't successful because I dictated *how* they demonstrated their learning. In some instances, we don't have a choice: if I am addressing a writing expectation in Language Arts, for example, my students need to write something, and if they haven't mastered effective writing, then they will not be successful. I would never suggest that we give students a false sense of their own accomplishments or abilities. But when my curriculum says "demonstrates an understanding of" or "can apply," then I don't have to give my students a writing task; in fact, the way kids demonstrate their learning does not even have to be the same. Dr. Catlin Tucker, among other educational leaders, speaks to the benefits of choice boards as a way to differentiate products or performance in order to "encourage higher rates of completion and more robust finished products."[10] What a shift this was for me! Instead of evaluating thirty of the SAME essays, I was able to evaluate thirty different products with the same learning outcomes. Yes, it was much more interesting for me, but more importantly, it allowed my students to use their strengths to show me what they had learned.

Some created videos, some infographics, some 3-D models, some interactive presentations. When I first started offering this, I wondered if it was fair for students who spent hours editing a movie versus the time it took to create an infographic. But this is where the reflection on their mistakes comes in. I would ask students to reflect on whether they made the right choice for their assignment and what they would do differently next time. The result of this practice meant that students met with greater success because they were choosing how to demonstrate their learning *and* they were reflecting on their "fails" and the effectiveness of their choices. The more I experimented with choice boards for differentiated products, the better I became at them.

There are a plethora of resources and templates out there (check out our resources at jcasatodd.com).

A FOCUS ON PEER FEEDBACK

Karen says that opportunities for peer review have been helpful. According to John Hattie's work on high-impact strategies and a meta-analysis of several studies, feedback has an exceptionally high effect size of success (ranked 10 out of 150) when it comes to student achievement. Peer tutoring and peer influence are ranked as 34 and 41 out of 150, respectively.[11] Peer feedback gets a bad rap because as Karen aptly suggests, kids don't necessarily know how to provide effective feedback to others. This is a sentiment shared by my own children and students, who share the opinion that peer feedback is a waste of time. When done right, however, peer feedback has tremendous benefits. According to the University of Oxford, peer feedback enables students to "better self-assess themselves as well as exposing them to different ways of approaching a task."[12] If kids look at feedback as an integral part of learning, they will be more likely to take a risk the first time.

The tell, ask, give (TAG) feedback method is a popular feedback structure similar to the Glow, Grow structure shared by Karen. TAG helps students deliver feedback to their peers in a way that's kind and effective. The general structure works with all levels of students, so it's easy for educators to tweak it according to the level of sophistication of feedback they want from students. Below are some sentence starters for TAG feedback:

<u>Tell</u>
Something you like:
- I like how you...
- I enjoyed... because...

<u>Ask</u>
A thoughtful question:
- How might you...?
- What did you mean when you said...?

Give
A positive suggestion:
- One suggestion I have is...
- You may want to change...

Mari Venturino, an educator and Google Certified Innovator and Trainer, has used the TAG structure as a springboard to develop a Google form with conditional formatting to help students better deliver the TAG feedback to one another.[13]

During presentations, I invite students to identify the strengths and weaknesses they see in the presentation on a quick Google Form that I later share with the presenters. Whenever I can, I implement a ranking system for peer feedback. When students presented their climate change prototypes to the class (you will hear more about that later), I not only asked their peers to identify strengths and areas for improvement, but I also asked them what they would have done differently. This last question emphasizes that even after the final product is submitted, there is room to reflect on the choices students made and

---

Strengths

Short answer text

Things that could be improved

Long answer text

I'd invest!! This innovation or invention...was presented well and might actually work!

	1	2	3	4	5	6	7	8	9	10	
Would not support with my $	○	○	○	○	○	○	○	○	○	○	Brilliant

Google Form feedback

the impact of those choices; it puts students in charge of their own learning. I will often put on a mock presentation and ask them to use the same evaluation on me. This helps students learn how to provide better feedback in a low-risk way. It's not often kids get to evaluate their teacher, so they love this, and students have shared that it has helped them to understand what to look for in a presentation.

Mark Gardner, in the Edutopia article "Teaching Students to Give Peer Feedback," suggests the SPARK strategy, which looks like this:

- **S**pecific: Comments are linked to something specific within the text.
- **P**rescriptive: Like a medical prescription, feedback offers a solution or strategy to improve the work, including possible revisions or links to helpful resources or examples.
- **A**ctionable: When the feedback is read, it leaves the peer knowing what steps to take for improvement.
- **R**eferenced: The feedback directly references the task criteria, requirements, or target skills.
- **K**ind: All comments must be framed in a kind, supportive way.[14]

Whether you use TAG or SPARK or any type of sentence prompts, I love tools that allow students to respond to others orally and in particular teach them how to respectfully disagree with others. Prompts can look like the following:

- I can see why you would say... but have you thought about...
- I respectfully disagree with the point ___ because...
- I agree with when you said... but I don't agree with...

The more we can explicitly teach and scaffold giving feedback, the better students will get at it.

MINECRAFT EDU

Almost a decade ago, I organized an EdTech day for teachers in my district and brought in some folks to talk about Minecraft Education and how it can be used in teaching and learning. As much as I loved the idea of it, I have to say that all the requirements and servers scared me! Today, you can use Minecraft Education on any device and the fees are per educator instead of per user, so it is very cost-effective. Inspired by my colleague Heather Chalmers, I took the plunge a few years ago and worked with countless geography classes ever since. I am going to be 100 percent honest with you, though: I cannot build anything in Minecraft! But the beauty is I don't have to because I ask kids who are proficient to be my tech-sperts. These students shine with pride; many of them would never consider themselves academic students or leaders. But I digress. The reason I am talking about Minecraft Education in this chapter is because it's a great tool for "failing forward." The Minecraft Teacher Academy lists six compelling reasons why Minecraft is effective in the classroom, so I created this slide to share with students.

Why Minecraft?

There are 6 reasons why we chose Minecraft as a tool for this unit:

- **Failure dynamic**-opportunities to fail forward
- **Flexibility Dynamic**-learning a variety of ways to solve a problem
- **Construction Dynamic**-building something that matters
- **Situated meaning**-learning new ideas by doing them
- **System thinking**-understanding how everything fits together
- **Building Empathy**-coming together to work together

Poll: How proficient are you with Minecraft?

1   2   3   4   5

Never   Epic Builder!

Students have to plan a sustainable city of their choosing, sketch it out, ask for feedback, and only then are they able to create their city in

Minecraft. The teachers and I have small group conferences and ask groups the following questions: What are your challenges? How are you overcoming them? Then, inevitably, one or two groups LOSE THEIR ENTIRE WORLD despite our warnings to export their worlds often and take screenshots as they go. You would think that this would be a teacher's nightmare: parents would complain, and students would be devastated. In some cases, all of these are true, but we go back to the slide we shared about why we chose Minecraft to begin with and have kids determine a solution. Some kids start all over again and create a simplified version, while others pivot and create a video based on the screenshots they took. When they present to the class, they begin with, "We lost our world and so...," and we make a point of sharing how proud we are of them for their resiliency and creativity after this happened. Each time I have worked on this project with students (over three hundred kids so far), I have given them them an additional opportunity to reflect on the unit by asking them what they are most proud of and to talk about their challenges and how they overcame them. Here is an example of one:

> Our group faced a few challenges while doing this assignment. One being that one of our group members was not able to join the minecraft world with the rest of us. This was a challenge because since one person could not join our minecraft world, it left the two of us to build the city ourselves. Then we came up with the idea that she would make her own world and build some of the city, while we in the other world would build the rest together. We then recorded our city together, and took a screenshot of the other city and put it on our slideshow.

Challenges

As frustrating as the failures are for students in the moment, they are almost always proud of how they rallied forward.

A FOCUS ON CRITICAL THINKING AND CREATIVITY

Garfield Gini-Newman, one of the senior consultants at The Critical Thinking Consortium, states that critical and creative thinking are intricately linked. He suggests that creativity in and of itself is quality thinking. He states that there are two steps in creativity: 1) fluency or the generation of new ideas and 2) merit or identifying which ideas are the most useful.[15] In the video "Creativity: The Science Behind the Madness," neuroscientist Wendy Suzuki suggests that most creative people use both the left and right parts of the brain, and psychologist Scott Barry Kaufman affirms that creativity requires both intelligence and imagination.[16] This is interesting, because when I think of creativity, I think I confuse it with artistry, so as an English teacher, asking kids to create a poem, song, or story may seem like the only way I could ask kids to practice creativity. Sir Ken Robinson defines creativity as "the process of having original ideas that have value," which "more often than not comes about through the interaction of different disciplinary ways of seeing things."[17] We need to ask ourselves this: How might we use critical thinking moments as opportunities for creativity, considering the broad range of student interests and needs in our classrooms?

We often host timed cardboard challenges in the library, in which we challenge kids to create the tallest tower with only straws and a bit of Play-Doh, create obstacles with Sphero robots, and make the most aerodynamic paper airplanes (on May 26, which is National Paper Airplane Day). None of these are connected to a particular subject, although they could be, and some of them require materials and prep time.

It's easy to think of critical and creative thinking as an afterthought or an "extra," but it is easy enough to make critical/creative thinking a regular practice in our classes because the skills don't actually require "stuff." These are a few prompts that can easily be incorporated into any content area that challenge kids to use their creative problem-solving skills:

- If ____ (the word "obstinate," "an obtuse triangle," "friendship") was a color, what color would it be?
- What would happen if...?
- How can you create a scenario for how ____, ____, and ____ are connected?
- Rank these (ideas, concepts, problems) from 1–10 and explain why that is the best order.

"Which one of these doesn't belong?" is another strategy that can be incorporated into any subject area fairly regularly. Students look at a variety of different graphics or items and determine which one does not belong, having to justify their responses.

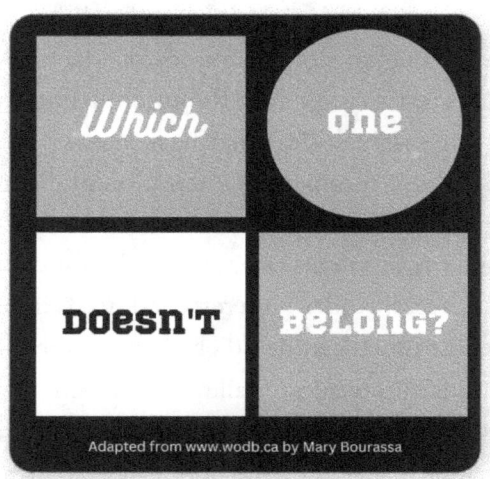

Which one doesn't belong?

There is no right or wrong answer because there are a variety of interpretations. It could be a series of graphs, maps, math problems, words, superheroes, etc. Such a critical thinking activity provides a quick but impactful way to show kids that there are multiple ways of solving a problem. It also encourages creativity, guesses, and hypotheses, and forces students to justify their answers with reasoning while providing a risk-free way to make mistakes.

VERTICAL, NONPERMANENT SURFACES

Peter Liljedahl, author of *Building Thinking Classrooms*, spoke to a group of teachers planning for a new destreamed curriculum in Ontario. One of the fourteen practices he talked about as most effective not just for thinking but for risk-taking was having kids engage in a thinking task at a vertical, nonpermanent surface. According to Liljedhal's research:

> One of the most enduring institutional norms that exists in mathematics classrooms is students sitting at their desks (or tables) and writing in their notebooks. This turned out to be the workspace least conducive to thinking. What emerged as optimal was to have the students standing and working on *vertical nonpermanent surfaces (VNPSs)* such as whiteboards, blackboards, or windows. It did not matter what the surface was, as long as it was vertical and erasable (nonpermanent). The fact that it was nonpermanent promoted more risk-taking, and the fact that it was vertical prevented students from disengaging. Taken together, having students work, in their random groups, on VNPSs had a massive impact on transforming previously passive learning spaces into active thinking spaces where students think, and keep thinking, for upward of 60 minutes.[18]

The other reason this works so well is that kids can look at what other kids are doing, thus further reducing the risk of looking foolish in front of their peers. You can call this cheating, but I think getting ideas from others in this way can also be considered peer tutoring. I proceeded to have frequent lessons begin with a thinking task at a vertical, nonpermanent surface, and I really noticed a change in student confidence and class dynamics. Having said that, a few students shared that standing up and being visible to others, while possibly humiliating themselves in front of other students (a constant worry in high school), actually stopped their learning. And so, like any strategy, knowing your learners and using a variety of strategies makes the most sense.

IDEA SPOTLIGHT
JOYFUL PRODUCTIVE STRUGGLE AND THE QUESTION MATRIX

A core value that has made a significant impact on my students' ability to fail forward with confidence has been an effort to teach joyful and productive struggle in my second-grade classroom. Productive struggle is the idea that teachers plan for discourse, problem solving, and collaboration around an obstacle. Students are given time and tools to grapple with conjectures, discuss strategies, and use trial and error to solve problems. But what happens when young children run into error after error, mistake after mistake? I was searching for a tangible resource that could be used to investigate a mistake and keep joyful learning progressing.

My leadership team had shared a resource called the Question Matrix. The Question Matrix, developed by Chuck Wiederhold, is a set of question starters designed to develop higher-order thinking.[19] I was interested in the possible deeper connection between inquiry and productive struggle and decided to try using the Question Matrix whenever I noticed students approaching that threshold of mistake-making vulnerability. The matrix is simple to use: Pair a vertical question with a horizontal question, then aim for a question that would land in the green quadrant because those are the most helpful. For example, *"What can I say for sure right now?"* Or *"How might I solve this problem another way?"*

One afternoon last spring, a group of my students were working on a mapmaking project. They had been designing a map of the playground and were struggling to find an effective way to divide up the work and agree on the size of the map. I reminded the group that they could grab a copy of the Question Matrix and see if they could ask some questions that could move the group past its growing impasse. One student began, "What would be the benefits of a small

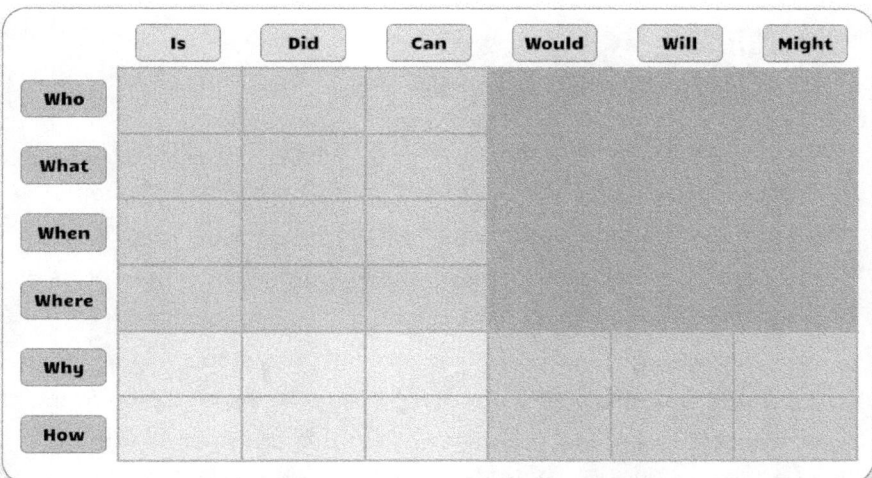

Question Matrix chart

map versus a large map?" The group began discussing and slowly came to agree that a large map would be more effective. "How will we all draw on the paper all at once?" a girl in the group asked next. Quickly the students began designing a turn-taking schedule for the parts of the map they would each be responsible for and in what order. The tone of the group changed. Students were empowered to move past the breakdown of mistakes and disagreement with a tool that was also teaching them a valuable skill set.

Teaching students to utilize the Question Matrix emboldens ownership over student problem solving. It has helped the students

in my classroom to feel more comfortable with making mistakes because they know that asking questions creates a path out of the "trouble." They also feel encouraged knowing that our class values time spent on this journey of joyful productive struggle.

LINDSAY WERNER, SECOND GRADE TEACHER

IDEA SPOTLIGHT
EMPHASIZE FAILING VERSUS FAILURE

When my students were doing the 20% Project (Genius Hour) in my class, we had an Epic Fail Board (inspired by a number of people) where they would pin up some of their biggest fails and epic risks.

The 20% Project required each student to challenge themselves. They were learning and creating with a purpose, often with lofty expectations and goals, and failing came at every step.

In the first month of the project, I could sense hesitation from many students who did not want to give 100 percent effort with the possibility of 90 percent failure. The Epic Fail Board changed the classroom culture from one that shied away from trial and error to one that supported and even celebrated risk-taking.

> I know there are many different definitions of "failing," but as a class, we adopted a mantra: "Sometimes you win, and sometimes you learn."

I've kept this as a personal mantra over the years as I left the classroom to become a K–12 instructional coach, director of technology, director of learning and innovation, UPenn GSE PLN faculty member, and now a business owner. I've also used this in my personal and professional life as an author, speaker, husband, and father.

Failing, it seems, is part of the job. Admitting that you've struggled is one thing. Sharing how you've struggled and learned is what matters. And so yearly, I write my own "Fail-ure Report"—I've since changed it to "Fail-ing."

I often talk about skateboarding when I talk about the difference between failure and failing. There's a big difference: when you're at a skate park and you fall down, it's celebrated. People expect you to fail and get back up and try again; in fact, your friends are there videoing, watching you fail time and time again. There's a video I show of a skateboarder falling several times before he lands the trick. It is not only celebrated but praised and supported by everybody in the community that failing is part of the process of learning how to skateboard, learning a new trick and getting back up and trying again.

When you expect failure to be part of the process, it's actually kind of fun. Learning is contagious if we allow the right environments to play. Students, kids, and all of us need to ultimately get to a level of success in something that is hard, challenging, and rigorous. Failing doesn't have a finality to it, because it's part of the growth. Failure does. I know it's a short and minimal change between the two words, but think about how you use them when you're talking to kids and when you're talking to yourself, and it will impact the way you change your fixed mindset to a growth mindset. It's a small change to a powerful word, but I hope you never use the "ure" at the end of "fail" again and always use the "ing" to make sure you keep on moving and keep on finding success through those small iterations of highlighting and improving. Here's to failing the next time you want to learn something! [20]

A.J. JULIANI, CEO, ADAPTABLE LEARNING, AND
WALL STREET JOURNAL **BEST-SELLING AUTHOR**

DISCUSSION QUESTIONS

1. If standardization continues to be a reality, what practices within the classroom counterbalance this?
2. Are there opportunities to implement more opportunities to fail forward within your context? What impact might this have on student attitudes toward mistakes? How will you know?
3. Where do you currently use peer review? How might you add more opportunities for peer review?
4. What is one idea from this chapter that resonates?

CHAPTER 2
GRADES

FROM THE STUDENT'S DESK: KAREN

I was the kid who always went the extra mile in elementary school. In sixth grade, my teacher assigned us an idiom to research every week, and one of the tasks was to find the origin of the idiom. While many students did the necessary amount of research, I filled up the front and back of our worksheet with all of my notes and provided in-depth explanations of the history of the idiom, even sharing multiple suspected origins.

One of the idioms we learned about was "caught red-handed." While writing this, I googled its origin to refresh my memory. As I learned in my past research, this idiom was used in fifteenth-century Scotland to describe a murderer caught with blood on their hands. I was surprised to see how many sources stated this—I found the answer in seconds because it was the first result that popped up on Google. In sixth grade, almost a decade ago, I had to do so much digging to find this answer. These idiom worksheets were meant to be brief and fun little exercises, but I didn't mind spending half an hour scouring the internet for the origin of Monday's idiom. I didn't want to settle for the first answer that came up because there was a possibility that might not be the best one. I always wanted to submit my best work.

I also liked annotating and analyzing literature in sixth grade. I'm a reader and writer at heart, so I always wrote more than what we had to write. Once, I received an award at the school assembly for the effort I put into my assignments. I never went the extra mile to be "better" than everyone else—I did it because the history of the idiom "caught red-handed," Langston Hughes's poems, and the novel *The View from Saturday* were interesting to me. I wanted to dive deeper for my personal enrichment.

When I entered middle school in seventh grade, I put less effort into learning because that was when I was exposed to letter grades and GPAs. I wanted to maintain a 4.0 GPA throughout middle school, and the extra work it took to pursue learning the way I did in elementary school was a waste of my time. I thought all that energy should be going toward my academics, and if I knew how much energy was enough to get an A, that's all I was willing to put forth. I had this mentality throughout middle school and high school, and it paid off because on paper, I was always an excellent student.

In the latter half of my K–12 education, I believed grades were one of the most important things in my life. A lot of the time, they were the most important—more important than my family, friends, and health. I was surrounded by excellent students. I had to be just as excellent to get into college, and my academics reflected my excellence—my self-worth. If I had the opportunity to do high school all over again, I would still choose grades over learning. But as I share in this chapter, I now realize how this was detrimental to my curiosity and growth. School could be so much more meaningful if grades were de-emphasized in the classroom so learning comes first for students.

GRADES HARM LEARNING

Is school about learning? Or is it about passing? For me, it's the latter, and it's because of grades. School should be about learning, something enjoyable and engaging we do to expand our minds. With grades in the picture and the constant pressure to get straight As, everything I do in school boils down to what percentage I'll end up with, so why learn and engage with the nonlinear path associated with learning?

Academic, author, and lecturer Alfie Kohn claims that grading is "inherently problematic" in his article "The Case against Grades." Grades, Kohn wrote, deter students from learning for learning's sake because grades generally do three things: reduce students' interest in learning, invite students to find the easy way out, and cause students to think less.[1]

All of these points apply to me. Getting As is the end goal, so the continuous, cumulative, and exciting process of learning is either nonexistent or short lived because I tap out once I get the grade I want. When my classes became remote during junior year of high school due to the COVID-19 pandemic, I didn't attend class the rest of the semester and submitted assignments late, if I did them, because I already had straight As. My district had a "hold harmless" grading policy wherein your grade couldn't be lower than what it was the last day of in-person instruction. That day, I had straight As. I was going to get straight As no matter what. Instead of continuing to work and engage, I took a break.

You could consider the lack of effort I put into learning to be cheating the system. Grades are seen as indicators of mastery and student progress. I'm a top student, so you'd think I'd be able to tell you a lot about the content in my classes, but I can't. I become an expert in the subject the night before an exam because I cram everything, but then I dump it all out of my brain once I hit Submit. (I think this is why I struggled in my high school math classes. My habit of memorizing, testing, and forgetting made it difficult for me to master the basics and have a good foundation in algebra, yet it eased my mental load.)

Kohn's second conclusion regarding grades is that they invite students to find the easy way out, and he says this doesn't mean students are lazy. It means they're rational, and I agree with him.[2]

What helped me not go insane from all the stress of school and getting good grades was this mantra: "Memorize, test, forget." I went to class with the mentality that I was there to get an A, so I should put my energy into doing just that. I didn't want to engage more than was needed to get an A because I had at least five classes to worry about at a time. The easy thing about taking AP classes was if I said what the College Board believed was the right answer, I knew I'd get an A. That was all it took to complete the assignment and move on. I'm aware I cheated myself out of connecting with the content the way my teachers might've wanted me to. At the end of the semester, I made up answers to the question "How did you grow in this course?" But again, I wouldn't do anything differently. Prioritizing my grades over learning helped me survive.

I worked hard to earn my grades, and I'm not going to downplay that. When I got home from school, I had some time to eat. Then at 2:00 p.m., my mom dropped me off at the local library on her way to work. After I spent four to six hours working and studying, my dad or grandpa picked me up, and it'd be dark outside. I remember sneaking snacks in the library because we couldn't eat inside. Eventually, I stopped doing that because I didn't have time to eat. My grades gave me academic validation and helped me get into college. If I had the opportunity to do high school all over again, I wouldn't do anything differently. Graduating in the top 10 percent of my class of over eight hundred students was worth the sleep deprivation–induced eye twitching and anxiety-induced dizziness.

In hindsight, however, I don't think grades mean much, and I am sad that I struggle to recall the content I learned in high school because I chose not to engage with it on a level that was deep and meaningful to me. I believe grades are an ambiguous measurement of academic performance and mastery. What my high school grades do a better job of measuring is how well I followed the directions on my assignments and regurgitated the lecture slides on an exam, and how much I exhausted myself. I still get good grades in college and like the academic validation, but I don't have much of an emotional attachment to my grades anymore because of this realization. I find it is now easier to pick myself up and move on from a bad grade.

THE PHYSICAL AND MENTAL TOLL OF GRADES

As Kohn and many researchers and education activists have found, grades not only inhibit learning but also contribute to an unhealthy academic culture. Grades were the center of my world in high school. I'm sure they are for many students and their families too.

While there are plenty of students who opt for easier classes to protect their GPA (an example of what Kohn meant when he said grades cause students to take fewer risks and learn less), there are also plenty of students who overload their schedule with Advanced Placement, International Baccalaureate, and honors classes to boost their GPA. I took three AP courses my junior year of high school alongside a community college course. My senior year, I took four.

Most advanced courses require students to do hours of studying and homework outside the classroom due to the fast pace and rigorous content. I consider myself to have excellent time management skills and a strong work ethic, but being inundated with readings, essays, and exams to study for led me to work into the evening and sometimes past midnight. Not to mention that many high school students have commitments outside of school. Countless of my peers in high school stayed up late regularly—or even pulled all-nighters—and got far less than the recommended seven to eight hours of sleep to finish doing homework and studying for all of their classes. Even if an assignment was worth a measly ten points, we stayed up late to get it done because it still affected our grades.

My high school yearbook surveyed two hundred seniors (our senior class was eight hundred total students) and found that 48 percent of the respondents reported sleeping between four to seven hours on average, with 5.5 percent saying they were sleeping less than four hours on average. And 43.5 percent of these seniors reported sleeping seven to nine hours on average, and 3 percent—only six students—said they were sleeping greater than nine hours on average. Even though there were a good number of students getting the recommended hours of sleep on average, let's not ignore that over half of these two hundred students were not sleeping enough. I'm part of that half—typically, I went to sleep by 1:00 a.m. and had to be up at 6:30 a.m. to make it to zero period in time.

Sleep deprivation isn't a problem unique to my school. A study published in 2018 analyzed data from the 2015 Youth Risk Behavior Survey (YRBS). According to the national 2015 YRBS for high school students in the United States, approximately 73 percent of these adolescents experienced short sleep duration, or less than eight hours of sleep for teens aged thirteen to eighteen.[3] Sleep deprivation brings about a variety of physical health issues, from increased risk of obesity to poor focus and concentration. Regular lack of sleep can also severely affect one's state of mind and worsen existing mental health issues.

There are numerous reasons why teenagers aren't getting the amount of sleep they need, science writer Eric Suni wrote for the Sleep Foundation. Some factors that affect sleep are school start times, electronic device usage, existing medical conditions, and, of course, busy schedules and workloads. Ironically, the sleep students sacrifice to secure high grades can be linked to academic performance. Students who regularly lose sleep have trouble focusing and retaining information, which hurts them in school.[4]

And sleep isn't the only aspect of health that students sacrifice for their academics. Many of my friends have said they struggle to find time to exercise and neglect their diet, even going so far as ignoring their need to eat in order to get their work done. I quit playing field hockey during my junior and senior years of high school because I had too much schoolwork. It wasn't an easy decision. Despite our intense practices and tough games, I looked forward to that time of the day when I was done with classes and headed off to play field hockey for a couple of hours. It was fun to be around my teammates—I had a group of friends on and off the field, and I also liked being physically active. I was in the best shape of my life when I played field hockey. Outside of field hockey, I wasn't that active because I was sitting down a lot to work. After quitting field hockey, I lost a part of my day dedicated to being around girls my age and unwinding through exercise because I was so busy with school. If I wasn't doing work, I spent my time thinking of the work I'd need to do soon or stressing about something school-related. I oftentimes feel I have to sacrifice my physical and mental well-being to succeed academically.

AN INTERLUDE: MISTAKES AND CHEATING

The fear of making mistakes is one of many contributors to cheating. Students cheat because of the pressure to do well and because making mistakes results in emotional and academic agony that can be hard to recover from. A lot of people say that cheating is the easy way out and is something only "lazy" and "stupid" students do. But high- achieving students also cheat.[5]

It's widely acknowledged that cheating is bad and can lead to severe consequences. So what's the response? Lockdown browsers, plagiarism detectors, eye-tracking software. But those don't address how the pressure to not make mistakes pushes students to cheat in the first place.

Howie Hua, a math professor at Fresno State University in California, posted on social media that despite having his students "sign an honor code saying they are only allowed to look at their notes and our videos, AND they can revise until they earn an A, I'm still not creating an environment where they can be honest with their work."[6]

Efforts at preventing cheating are better directed toward creating an environment that teaches students the value of mistakes and does not severely punish students for making them. In doing so, we take sustained and direct action toward creating an environment where students feel comfortable and supported and do not feel suffocated in a meaningless pursuit of perfection.

STUDENT SPOTLIGHT

I have always been a straight A student looking for the next step. Throughout my school career, I have constantly looked for the next bar to hit. Something to fulfill my extremely high expectations. That is why when it came to grades, they would hang over my head as a constant reminder that I can't stop. I may be able to maintain a 4.0, but something about not being perfect lingers in my head like an old perfume. A singular drop in percentage would be heartbreaking, but not without good reason. Obsessing over grades also means that I work extremely hard to maintain them. Anything less than 90 percent is disappointing. I need to remind myself that a grade is simply a number on a page. In some circumstances, it can reflect how much effort you put into a specific subject; however, in no way should it ever determine your intelligence level. If I could go back to when my obsession started, I would step away from my work and choose to be present *and* proud. Grades should not hold immense importance; as long as I am putting effort into my passions, I will continue to have pride.

A significant factor that I have found helps students be present is to foster active learning and generally have a positive attitude toward the material. Little things like group discussions and problem-solving tasks can go a long way. This also pairs with a teacher's actions in the classroom. As a student, I can often feel overwhelmed with new material, but I have grown to adore the teachers who approach these challenges with a positive mindset and set a good example for their students when it comes to learning. In terms of being proud, I enjoy teachers who work with their students. Even if the 90s is not an obtainable goal, being able to see improvement within in-class subjects is what often helps students feel most proud of their work. This once again ties back into being encouraging and providing assistance on a more personal level (which I know is extremely hard, especially in high school, but even getting feedback from the class as a whole can help). The most memorable time in which I prioritized my learning instead of a number was my first experience in ninth grade English. I am very much not language-oriented, and I struggled extremely hard with analyzing and putting my thoughts into words. However, I am so glad I went through that experience. I stopped stressing about what I felt was proper to put on the page and focused on what I could gather. I didn't improve immediately, but having those failures and feedback is what helped me formulate better paragraphs and truly understand the concepts.

ISABELLA F., TENTH GRADE, ONTARIO, CANADA

WHAT WORKS FOR ME

Grades held a tremendous amount of weight throughout my education. Without grades, I believe students would be liberated from the chains that keep our imagination at bay. We would stop trying to be so perfect, desperate, and fearful all the time. We would be more involved in our learning, and in doing so, explore the unknown and take risks and experiment and fail and get back up more often.

Kohn points out in his article "The Case against Grades" that criticisms of grading have existed for decades. He writes that looking back on the early criticisms of grades "remind[s] us just how long it's been clear there's something wrong with what we're doing as well as just how little progress we've made in acting on that realization."[7] Kohn's article was published in 2011, and we are having the same conversations in 2025 because our education system has seen minimal changes in regard to grading.

While I advocate for the elimination of grades across the school system because I believe they hinder students' learning, that doesn't seem likely anytime soon because of how deeply entrenched grades are in both K–12 and higher education schooling systems as well as college admissions (and because of the tortoise-like pace of major changes in education). In spite of this challenge, there are still ways for teachers to de-emphasize grades in their individual classrooms and contribute to the larger movement against grades:

1. FOCUS ON LEARNING.

My AP English Language teacher, Mr. Ziebarth, avoided talking about grades as much as possible in his English and journalism classes. What he was more gung ho about were learning and growth, and he demonstrated this in various ways.

When we practiced writing introductions and thesis statements for our rhetorical essays, he had some students share their work with the rest of our class and gave live feedback. After every quick session of feedback, another student, who incorporated that feedback into their work right away, shared what they had written, and the process continued until the period ended. The rubric Mr. Ziebarth used wasn't a long, robust, and intimidating checklist that had students losing their minds over making sure they'd done everything perfectly. Instead, a large part of his rubric asked students to be truthful and surprising in their writing, which encouraged creativity and risk-taking in order to create something that's out of the box. Whenever he talked about grades, he always reminded us that they're not something we should obsess over and that he cared more about us learning than about what grade we ended up with.

Mr. Ziebarth's methods transformed his classroom into a space to learn because he made grades the least of our worries. Vanessa Ellis, an eighth-grade social studies teacher at Veterans Memorial Middle School in Columbus, Georgia, also shared how changing her language helped her change her students' mindsets from grade-obsessed to learning-obsessed.

"I evolved my language to emphasize learning, not grades, mastery instead of points, progress rather than perfection," Ellis wrote in her post "Not Yet Gradeless, but Grading Less" for the blog *Teachers Going Gradeless*.[8]

Some of the questions Ellis encouraged her students to ask in the classroom were "How can I show improvement?" and "I don't quite understand this topic yet. Are there additional resources available to help me learn this better?" She wrote that she saw her students develop growth mindsets and take "actions to improve their learning."

2. PROVIDE WRITTEN OR VERBAL FEEDBACK AND MINIMIZE GRADING WHEN POSSIBLE.

Grades and rubrics are often cold and impersonal to me, whereas feedback is unique to each student and lets them know what they did well and where they need to improve. Students might not need or want feedback on a five-point worksheet, but they want it on larger projects and papers. In my personal experience, however, when grades are involved, sometimes feedback falls short because the grade carries too much weight and distracts me from learning. It would help to minimize grades as much as possible when delivering feedback.

During larger assignments in language arts and social studies classes, it's possible to break these assignments into chunks and for the grading of prewriting assignments to be based on completion, if grading is required. With a minimal emphasis on grades during the prewriting and revision process, teachers can truly drill feedback and the importance of learning into their students and see them thrive and master the standards they need to. This is the exact structure of my first-year writing classes in college.

In a humanities course I took, my professor assigned a prewriting assignment that helped my classmates and me outline our paper. We wrote our preliminary thesis, chose what we were going to analyze, found evidence, and more. These prewriting assignments counted toward our participation grade, and we'd get 100 percent if we completed them. I found the entire writing process—prewriting, writing, and revision—to be far less stressful than it was in high school despite each essay being worth 35 percent of our grade. The writing process was low-stakes, so instead of me worrying so much about my grade, I felt like I had the mental and emotional capacity to focus more on the feedback I was receiving on my prewriting and applying it to my essay.

A writing course I took had a blog component in which we wrote three blog posts each quarter. Similar to the writing process for essays, my professor graded our blog post submissions based on completion. He gave us feedback on our blog posts through Canvas or during office hours, and he expected us to revise our website throughout the quarter with his feedback. Then, at the end of the quarter, he looked at our entire website again and finally gave us an actual grade. This was a great way of removing the stress from a quarter-long project and helping students grow.

I know this grading method is difficult to implement in math classes. Many math classes are assessment-intensive because it's critical to ensure that students master the content they were taught before learning higher-level math concepts. With math tests, it's hard to deliver feedback because in many cases, you either know or don't know the material. In "How to Create a Gradeless Math Classroom in a School That Requires Grades," Andrew Burnett's feedback-based assessment called Show Me What You Can Do has improved students' math skills and made them more focused on hitting learning targets.[9] Relatedly, "A Year of Mathematical Freedom" by educator Abe Moore is about the outcomes and successes of "mathematical freedom" in his classroom.[10]

FROM THE TEACHER'S DESK: JENNIFER

I don't think that a single teacher would disagree with the idea that grades and the pursuit of grades prevent kids from learning. But here's the reality. Most of us work within a system where a huge emphasis is placed on standardized testing, and grades and reporting are expectations upon which our jobs in large part depend. Despite my best intentions (literally every year I say, "This year will be different!"), I inevitably fall back into the trap of grading EVERYTHING! For some reason, I bought into the mindset that kids won't complete the work if it isn't being evaluated. I also found that I give so many assignments that I grade, but then the actual weight of the assignment is so minimal that it doesn't do anyone any good. In Canada, our exam period often falls during the Super Bowl. My husband, a lover of the Green Bay Packers, would often host friends or we would get invited to a Super Bowl viewing party; I do not recall a single party where I did not have a pile of essays to mark. I have vivid memories of sitting in a corner trying not to get nachos on the essays I brought with me to grade. Many weekends, I would bring home my pile of marking only to bring it back unevaluated on Monday morning with an incredible guilt weighing upon me. I would appease my guilt by promising my students donuts if I didn't give them back their papers by an arbitrary date I set. Don't worry, I am shaking my head about how ridiculous that was, too! A favorite story my husband likes to tell is one in which I decided to follow some advice I saw online: stand up while grading papers to avoid falling asleep. When I tried that, while grading *Macbeth* essays, the result was that I literally fell asleep while standing by the dishwasher. My husband ran into the kitchen when he heard a thud; we still have the indentation in our dishwasher as a reminder!

When I think about moments in my teaching career when I wanted to walk away from teaching even though I love it, it is because I was overwhelmed and exhausted by the pile of papers I had to grade.

Karen's comments about cheating really resonated as well. How often have I seen it in my career? A student so desperate for a good grade that they plagiarized an essay even when I had explicitly shared exactly what constitutes academic dishonesty. When I read Karen's rationale for the fact that many students cheat because they are afraid of failure, it made me pause. Obviously, this was true for her and her experience, but it made me think of another reason, one that a student named Alex taught me several years ago. I was Alex's English teacher for two years. In that time, we studied several class novels. I assigned oodles of homework questions (we'll talk more about homework in a later chapter), and I never remembered Alex not doing his homework. He also always handed in assignments, and although he wasn't getting 90s, he achieved a low B in both tenth and eleventh grades. When he was in twelfth grade, I was no longer his English teacher, and I had moved into a special education resource role. I was now his core resource teacher. It was then that he admitted to me that he had never read a single novel in the two years he had me as a teacher. He also shared that he was able to get his assignments done and pass tests by befriending students who were "smarter": he basically learned how to cheat the system. This blew me away and made me angry, frustrated, and sad. He admitted he liked me as a teacher and liked how passionate I got about literature, but he said, "I just had to wait long enough, and you (or another classmate) would give me the answer." You may not call that cheating, but I think that the motivation to just cruise by without actually caring about learning anything is a reality for Alex and many other students in front of us. Add to this the fact that current artificial intelligence (AI) apps can easily facilitate shortcuts. At the time of writing this book, several AI tools can paraphrase, summarize, and create responses that may or may not be detected by plagiarism technology. We live in a time when, in literal seconds, AI can be prompted to "Write a winter-themed sonnet" or "Write a five-paragraph essay on the theme of appearance versus reality in George Orwell's *1984* using textual evidence." More about this tech and how we can use it to innovate in a later chapter.

Here are a few ideas from my own practice that address Karen's experiences.

PROCESS OVER PRODUCT

The term "assessment" in Latin is *assedere*, which means to "sit beside." When we place a greater emphasis on the product over the process, we lose the opportunity to focus on the learning that is happening.

The prewriting assignment Karen shares is a good example of how an assignment helped her with the final product. One of the stories I share in my chapter of *Because of a Teacher, Volume II*, edited by George Couros, is the idea shared by Damian Cooper and Jeff Catania, authors of *Rebooting Assessment*, about the value of process over product:

> He compared K12 school to flight school. He said, "The Air Canada pilot gets to 'redo' the landing hundreds of times before 'it counts.' It's called 'practice' and it occurs in the flight simulator. And those practices lead the prospective pilot to mastery. If we are implementing assessment correctly, it will actually lead to a raising of standards because poor-quality work is deemed unacceptable." This makes so much sense to me. Assessment should be about helping kids to master my own curriculum more than it is about preparing them for the next grade, a standardized test, or "the real world." I soon came to understand that the more I could "sit beside" students, the more they set their own goals, and the more I taught them to be reflective of themselves and others, the better they did on the summative pieces.[11]

The other value to process over product is that we can more readily see and understand what a child knows in a way that we can't on a test. For example, having book club conversations in small groups with students in my English classes allowed me to listen to what resonated with students in terms of themes and characters in a way that asking them multiple-choice questions could never do. I would certainly have noticed that Alex had not read any books if I had prioritized process over product!

SHARE THE FEEDBACK BEFORE THE GRADE

The idea that Karen and other students bring up about grades actually detracting from learning is also something that I have noticed in my career time and time again. As a high school English teacher, especially, I would spend hours grading essays only to have students toss the paper in the trash can after looking at the mark they got. I cannot tell you the fury I felt thinking about all of the precious hours I could have spent with my family. And so, on the recommendation of my colleague Kevin Woods, I stopped sharing the grade. The first time I did this, I thought the kids were going to revolt. "But what mark did I get?" and "Where's my mark?" ensued even after I explained to students that we were going to try something a little different. We had co-constructed the rubric so kids knew what the expectations for the assignment were. I also had a tendency of giving lots of feedback throughout the page. The new process was that I would give students the rubric and feedback and ask them to give themselves a mark based on my feedback. They would come to my desk and share what mark they thought they earned and why. Then I pulled out the rubric I had used to grade their paper or assignment and we compared notes. Sometimes, I would change the grade when the "why" gave me insight as to what the student learned. This became standard practice in my classroom, and interestingly, their self-assessed mark increasingly matched mine as students understood the criteria better and actually used my feedback for future assignments.

HAVE STUDENTS GRADE THEIR OWN WORK

My colleague Scott goes one step further. He shares the feedback and allows students to determine their own grade. When I first heard this, it didn't sit well with me. After all, I am the teacher. I should have that power. Wait a minute. *That power?* Yikes. Where did that come from? Actually, I think Scott is bang on. Students don't just come up with a grade out of thin air; they look at his feedback and reflect on their strengths and weaknesses. They also need to justify the grade they are giving themselves based on all of that information. In the twenty years Scott has been teaching, he has never had a negative interaction with a parent, has always gotten his report cards out on time, and has been one of the most beloved teachers. Last year, I tried it myself. We co-constructed the rubric and students had to identify what grade they would give themselves and why. They also had to indicate what they thought they did well for each curriculum expectation and what they could have done better. The co-teacher and I allowed for class time to do this. The result? The marks students gave themselves mostly matched the marks we would give them. When they did not, the ensuing conversation resolved the issue. Another result of this was that students found the process extremely difficult. I asked kids why they thought this, and they admitted they had never had to give themselves a mark before and didn't know how to do it. Clearly there is value in allowing students to grade themselves as a standard practice.

ALLOW MULTIPLE REVISIONS

As a teacher who sees ninety-plus students a semester (and has to grade all of their assignments), this idea actually sounds horrible! And yet... if I allow a student the opportunity to "try again" until they are happy with the result (even if it is a grade they are striving for), isn't this reinforcing the idea that practice makes perfect? Think of a skateboarder. Are they happy with a decent run, or do we often see them trying over and over to get it perfect? My messaging: "If you are not happy with your grade, and feel like you can do better, please let me know when I can expect a revised copy." Students had to hand in the original, the new assignment, and a note about what was different and why this change made their assignment better. When I gave this choice to my students, not many of them took me up on the offer, but knowing that the option was there shifted the me-versus-them notion to students recognizing that I wasn't out to get them, but that I wanted them to succeed. When I return the grade in our learning management system (in my case, Google Classroom), I do so with a variation of the following note:

Hello friends,

I have returned your work and posted your mark. If you review my feedback and would like to address the concerns, please send me a message and re-submit. I am happy to reassess your work if it is handed in before January 10th. Please highlight the changes you made next to my feedback.

Best, Ms. Casa-Todd

A few important things to note about this practice:

- I am always careful to add a deadline for accountability's sake and a note about highlighting the changes next to my feedback. I don't have time to reassess an entire product, and this helps streamline the assessment.
- The students who did choose to revise their work inevitably got a higher mark, and those who chose not to, well, that was their choice to make and they knew it.
- Students have shared that they felt like they were the ones in control of their own destiny (a.k.a. grade).

METACOGNITION AND ASSESSMENT

Karen shares how powerful it was for her to engage in peer assessment, and in the previous chapter we learned how important feedback was to her learning and growth. Metacognition, a form of self-assessment where students think about their thinking and learning, is a research-based strategy that helps students set goals for themselves and work toward their goals. The more we involve students in the process of assessment, the more students will become engaged in the learning versus the grade they receive. Having students evaluate themselves, as mentioned previously, is actually an exercise in metacognition. So, too, is having students co-construct rubrics. So often we give students checklists and rubrics without them really understanding them. One practice that works for me is to ask students to help me create a rubric, give students an example (it doesn't have to be an A—in fact, I prefer the exemplar to be a low B), and have them partner up to evaluate that exemplar using the rubric we created. We then talk about it. I ask students if the rubric makes sense and if we need to change it. I also ask them what the strengths of the product are and what would make this product better? This takes me about thirty minutes, and I have never regretted the time it has taken me to engage in this practice. In Ontario, this process is called "Assessment *AS* Learning" and involves students being actively engaged in their learning by focusing on the student as the connector between assessment and learning.[12]

After every unit, I list the expectations we covered and ask students what they were most proud of, what they felt like they needed to work on, and what goals they have for the next unit. I even ask them what they changed based on peer feedback. For this to be authentic, it took time to do properly, as I felt it was important to have students share their reflections with me in a mini-conference. But honestly, the old adage "Go slow to go fast" really applied here as the practice helped us to be on the same page and really targeted skills and goals.

When I first started teaching AP classes, I was really intimidated by parent–teacher interviews. I decided I would bring the students' metacognitive reflections to my meetings, and it was brilliant. After all, what parent could argue about the goals their own children set out? Doing this made every parent–teacher interview from that day forward more effective for all of us.

Mindset Works has created something called the "Effective Effort Rubric," which utilizes a growth mindset format as well as reflection prompts to get kids to think about their thinking and learning. Here is an example:[13]

Skill	Fixed	Mixed	Growth
Taking on Challenges	I avoid challenges whenever I can.	I take on challenges only when I have had some success with the challenge in the past.	I see challenges as a way to learn and grow. Bring on new challenges!

The rubric explicitly asks students questions about how well they accept feedback and criticism, practice strategies, ask questions, take on challenges, and focus on tasks.

Peer assessment is a skill that also needs to be taught and scaffolded and which can help students connect learning with assessment. In the previous chapter, we shared several methods for giving feedback. Increasing the frequency by which students give feedback to their peers, and teaching them explicitly how to do this, is a transferable skill they can use for the rest of their lives. Whether kids are creating an invention for climate change, an example of a sustainable city in Minecraft, or a five-paragraph essay, getting feedback from peers prior to handing in a final product allows students the opportunity to reflect on what they did well and what needs to be improved. At jcasatodd.com, you can access and modify templates for peer assessment and find additional sentence-starters posters for responding to peers as well.

IDEA SPOTLIGHT
THE SINGLE-POINT RUBRIC AND A GRADE PITCH

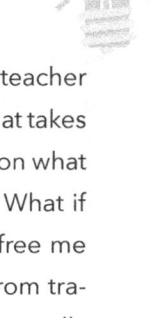

My gradeless learning journey started at the intersection of teacher burnout and the frustration that comes with the negotiation that takes place at the end of the marking period. What if I could focus on what I love (teaching and learning) and honor students' growth? What if I could do the heavy lifting during class time, which would free me up more outside class time? After some research, I shifted from traditional grading to gradeless by asking myself, "What are you really assessing?" I prioritized the Common Core Standards to focus on the standards that provided the most leverage for our grade-level skills. Prioritizing standards allowed me to focus on what students could do at the beginning of the semester (or trimester, or marking period), and help my students set goals for their reading and writing growth that they then tracked and reflected upon throughout our time together.

To provide feedback and help students reflect, I opted for a single-point rubric rather than a four-column, four-row rubric. Single-point rubrics are feedback focused, as there is a place to offer specific recognition of what students did well (glows) and feedback on what students want to improve upon (grows). This very specific feedback helps students to craft goals for their next extended response and track their own growth and development as writers, and it centers both me and my students in their work, instead of allowing the focus to become about justifying the grade or points-grabbing.

This is a snapshot of what the single-point rubric can look like:

Characterization Project Rubric

Glows What are the strong aspects of your work?	Outcome(s) What are the learning targets of this lesson/task(s)? I can:	Grows How can you strengthen your work for next time?
	Introduce a topic and main idea, organize complex ideas to make important connections and distinctions ❏ Exceeding ❏ Meeting ❏ Emerging	
	Explain and develop the topic with well-chosen, relevant, and sufficient details ❏ Exceeding ❏ Meeting ❏ Emerging	
	Apply sources and include citations for evidence ❏ Exceeding ❏ Meeting ❏ Emerging	

Single-point rubric

At the end of the marking period (trimester or semester), the students will complete a "grade pitch," where they explain, based upon the criteria outlined at the beginning of the course, what grade they would like to pitch and what supports their pitch. I provide students with questions to guide their grade pitch, I take notes on what they talked about in their pitch, and we discuss an appropriate grade that reflects their true growth and learning.

Although it has taken me several years to adjust my system as my understanding has changed, I will never return to traditional grading. As a veteran teacher, my understanding of the Common Core Standards, what I'm truly assessing, and true learning has allowed for more joyful learning experiences for both me and my students.

DEANNA LOUGH, READING SPECIALIST,
POSTLETHWAIT MIDDLE SCHOOL, CAMDEN, ME

IDEA SPOTLIGHT
STUDENT NAVIGATION TOOL

For years I watched my math students have difficulty connecting what they had already learned with what they were currently learning. Many of these same students also did not have a firm grasp of what they understood or what was giving them difficulty. I heard students say things like "I don't get it" or "I need help," but they were unable to verbalize where they were having difficulty. As a result, my students' understanding and grades suffered. Things changed for me and my students after I read a study by Professor Peter Liljedahl where he found an increase in engagement and an improvement in grades when students have the opportunity to see all of the skills they are learning in a unit and when they are given time to self-assess their understanding for what they have already learned. Based on this research, I developed a student navigation tool that shows students the different skills they will be learning throughout a unit along with sample questions associated with the skills. I begin each unit by handing out the navigation tool to students and have them tape it into their notebooks.

Here is an example of what this looks like:

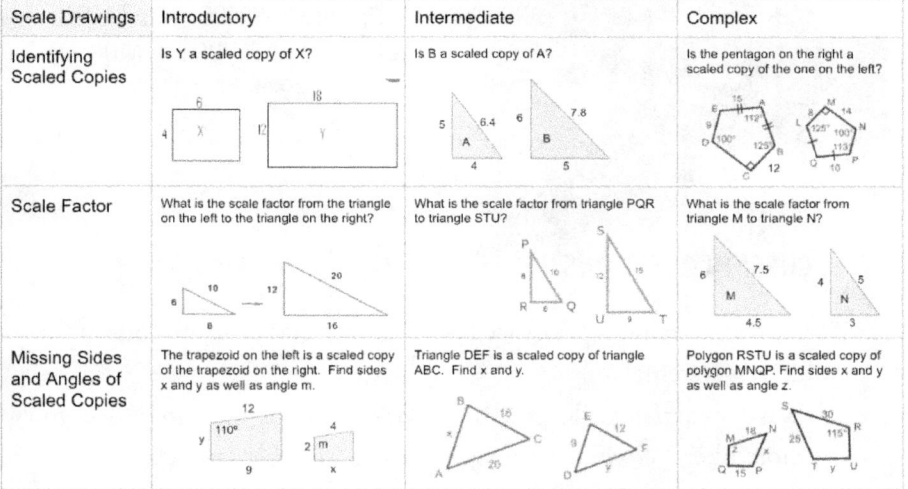

Student navigation tool

After teaching a lesson, I ask students to find the skill and the questions associated with that skill on the navigation tool. Next, I say to them, "If I were to give an assessment right now on this skill, how confident would you be in solving these questions?" Students self-assess their understanding by writing a "U" to represent "Understanding" or a "D" to represent "Developing Understanding" next to each question. Then I have them look back at skills that they have already self-assessed. I have them adjust their self-assessment if their understanding has changed, and I also ask them to find any connections to what they just learned. Finally, I ask students to look forward to the remaining skills that have not yet been taught and see

if they can determine where their learning will go next. This adjustment to my teaching has helped students better verbalize where they are having difficulty, and I have seen an improvement in their learning and engagement. Student grades have improved, and along with that, students have more confidence in math.[14]

ANDREW BURNETT, SEVENTH-GRADE MATH TEACHER, F. A. DAY MIDDLE SCHOOL, NEWTON, MA

DISCUSSION QUESTIONS

1. How can we help prioritize learning over grades within our grade-driven systems?
2. What experience do you have with students cheating? Are you more likely to see this among your higher-achieving students?
3. What opportunities for peer and self-assessment do you see in your own context?
4. What is one idea from this chapter that resonates?

CHAPTER 3

CONNECTIONS

FROM THE STUDENT'S DESK: KAREN

Despite my grievances about school, one of the best parts of it was the ethnic and cultural diversity among my classmates. I've heard countless stories on social media from those who are part of a racial or ethnic minority group about school being a terrible place. They talk about the microaggressions they experienced, such as their classmates teasing them for bringing "smelly" food or not speaking perfect English. Many have also spoken about how they denied their heritage and now regret being disconnected from their culture.

These stories made me realize how lucky I am to have always been in diverse classrooms. My schools embraced diversity among the student body. My high school, for instance, had several cultural clubs. They often shared their food, music, and more with the school community during our annual Spring Festival, which was planned by the Associated Student Body.

Multicultural events that celebrate the vibrant diversity of students promote school connectedness. The American Psychological Association defines school connectedness as "the belief held by students that adults and peers in the school care about their learning as well as about them as individuals."[1] Students who feel connected in school tend to have better relationships with their peers and teachers, succeed academically, and engage in healthy habits. I attribute some of my academic success to how my schools celebrated diversity because it created a welcoming environment. If I didn't feel accepted in school—where I spent at least seven to eight hours almost every school day for much of my youth—I probably would've been distracted and overwhelmed by the stress, anxieties, and insecurities and consequently struggled to stay engaged in class and build meaningful relationships with people around me.

Diversity, however, is only one part of school connectedness. The ways my K–12 schools addressed diversity to make the student body more connected generally made me feel good, but I still felt disconnected from my classmates and teachers in other ways. For example, the feeling of competition in my high school experience often led to conversations starting with "What did you get on..." and everyone comparing themselves to one another. We were each other's rivals instead of each other's companions. School should be a place where connections come first so we can learn and grow together.

COMPETITION HARMS CONNECTIONS

The classroom has always been a hypercompetitive environment for me, especially due to the pressure of grades, as discussed in chapter 2. In middle school, I could see my class rank in my math classes. This initially thrilled me and served as my motivation for working hard in my math classes because I loved being in the top three. But looking back, I now believe these class rankings are toxic—especially for thirteen- and fourteen-year-olds—and set me up to have poor and superficial relationships with my classmates in middle school and high school.

When my class rank was lower than I liked it to be, I felt resentful of my peers who ranked higher than me. They didn't do anything to harm me, but I was jealous, and I recall having these feelings as early as elementary school because my school had ranked the top three students who had earned the most Accelerated Reader points. I used to be first, but other students were better than me, and it led me to have ugly feelings that I don't think any elementary student should have to experience.

I didn't like that I was falling behind and no longer at the front of the pack. I also hated myself sometimes because I felt my self-worth and identity were tied to my academics. The number that motivated me to do my best was also the number that tore me down. It was the number I saw every day and the number that reminded me I wasn't the best and that maybe I didn't belong in my math class. Competition in school made my classrooms feel like a lonely place because I felt that all my peers and I cared about was ourselves and being at the top.

CONNECTIONS IN SCHOOL SUPPORT STUDENTS' WELL-BEING

My little sister puts up a fight every morning when she has to wake up at 7:00 a.m. to get ready for school—*just five more minutes, five more minutes!* She doesn't like going to school and doing her work, but at the end of the day, she doesn't want to leave and say bye to her friends. Hanging out with her friends is the best part of school for her, and that's something a lot of us can relate to because our friends make school fun. School is also one of the primary places for socialization for young children and adolescents. At school, we learn to communicate, be responsible, listen to teachers, and more. A lack of connections in school can harm mental health and learning, as evident in some of the effects of virtual instruction on students during the COVID-19 pandemic.

School took place in a fully remote environment for months during the pandemic. Online learning isn't for everyone because social interaction between students and teachers is limited, and sometimes the virtual instruction during the pandemic wasn't as structured or predictable as a traditional classroom. However, we didn't have a choice but to virtually teach and learn during the pandemic, and we also had to stop participating in most extracurricular activities. Some students thrived during online education, but many didn't because the remote environment made it hard for them to stay engaged in class and feel connected with their peers; it also disrupted their daily schedules. I enjoyed virtual school, which mostly took place during my junior and senior years of high school, but I couldn't see any of my friends. I missed having lunch with them and walking with a big group of classmates during passing period. It's also awkward to make small talk on Zoom, especially when everyone's camera is turned off. You can't have your typical private side conversations during online meetings, either. The pandemic reduced school to being just a place to teach and learn for me, and I think many of us can agree that school wasn't as fun because we couldn't form or maintain solid relationships with our colleagues and classmates. That's exactly what Ethan Davila, a student from New York, told the *New York Times*.

> I too believe that school is more than just academics alone. School is what makes the basis of our early lives, fourteen years of work, stress, and success. Not to mention all the great people you meet along the way, such as our mentors and teachers, as well as our lifelong friends. The activities I miss the most in school are going to my locker early in the morning, having quick chats with friends and colleagues, and roaming the halls listening to music. Afterschool activities are another story, I miss going to track practice, making jokes with friends on a local loop (1.5 mile run around campus), and getting a good workout in for the day (thanks Mr. Frazer).[2]

Connections and emotional intelligence are important, and being around our supportive friends and teachers is one of the best parts of being a student. Pew Research Center's June 2022 report on how teens navigated school during COVID-19 found that about one-third of teens said they felt less close to classmates (33 percent) or teachers (30 percent).[3] As a result of this disconnection, teens suffered in various ways; according to a *Washington Post* feature on Teen Line, founded in 1980, the support hotline was flooded with calls from teens during the pandemic. They were struggling with their mental health, relationships, families, and loneliness: "Most of the teens who called or texted were communicating the same message, in one way or another: *I feel so alone*. The pandemic had stolen so much, including the thing they wanted most: time with each other."[4]

Teaching and learning were also affected by a lack of school connectedness—Emily Barkley from New Jersey told the *New York Times* that there was "a significant lack of motivation" in a remote learning environment because of the limited peer-to-peer and teacher-to-peer interactions.[5] From a teacher's perspective, the struggle to connect with students in the classroom affected teachers' ability to deliver instruction and help their students.

High school math teacher Marianne Karp from Fountain Valley, California, said distance learning "tremendously affected" her teaching: "My greatest strength in reading faces of students that do not understand a concept has been stripped from me. The interactions with students going to the board and getting help from their classmates has been taken away as well. Losing that classroom culture of 'this class feels like home' has been rough for me."[6]

Discussions about increased school connectedness, building school culture, improving student–teacher relationships, and similar topics have been ongoing since even before the COVID-19 pandemic. In 2018, the Harvard Graduate School of Education published a two-part research story on school culture. They defined a strong school culture as one that is based on healthy connections, good communication, and positive traits and behaviors among members of the school community. Students who feel as if they belong in school also tend to perform well and engage academically: "Chantelle from Aurora, Canada, responded to a voluntary survey we conducted saying, 'Teachers improve my learning by being supportive and offering help and motivation. However they inhibit my learning when I don't feel welcome or supported.'"[7]

Researchers have also advocated for school connectedness by studying how school connectedness supports youth development. According to a 2010 literature review on school connectedness, "In general, researchers tend to view school connectedness on a continuum, with higher school connectedness associated with good outcomes and lower school connectedness associated with poor outcomes." It notes that elementary students tend to experience the highest level of school connectedness, while high school students experience the lowest level. In this literature review, Kathryn C. Monahan, Sabrina Oesterle, and J. David Hawkins assert that there are positive behavioral, emotional, and academic outcomes associated with school connectedness and that school connectedness should be prioritized in order to prevent students from experiencing maladaptive development such as engaging in unhealthy and dangerous behaviors.[8]

Dr. Robert W. Blum of Johns Hopkins University wrote in his 2005 article "A Case for School Connectedness" that teachers are "central" in encouraging school connectedness, adding that a supportive school administration is also needed:

> Teachers are obviously central to the equation. Although school connectedness might suggest smaller class sizes, the classroom's culture seems to matter more than its size does. Effective teachers can create connectedness in the classroom in a number of ways. When teachers make learning meaningful and relevant to their students' lives, students develop a stake in their own education. When teachers create a clear classroom structure with consistent expectations for behavior and performance, they provide a healthy setting in which students can exercise autonomy and practice decision-making skills. Teachers build connectedness in the classroom when they encourage team learning exercises. Cooperative learning tends to break down social isolation by integrating student teams across gender, academic ability, and ethnicity. Rewarding a variety of student achievements

and recognizing student progress—not only top performance—are also important components.[9]

There is still research being done on school connectedness. In 2019, for example, researchers published an article on the link between social media usage, school connectedness, and academic performance among adolescents, concluding that increased social media usage is inversely related to school connectedness and academic performance.[10] Scholars in 2020 found that students' connections to school are crucial in moderating adolescent suicidal behavior and students who are more connected to school are less likely to report suicidal behavior.[11] Moreover, ongoing research on the effects of COVID-19 and isolation on students makes it clear that schools need to prioritize school connectedness to help young people bounce back from the pandemic.[12] Students have personal struggles outside of school, and school itself is an incredibly stressful environment. Therefore, having a school environment that is welcoming, caring, and connected makes students feel safe and empowered during the many hours they spend at school each day.

WHAT WORKS FOR ME

Earlier in this chapter, I discussed why I felt like I belonged in school because there was ethnic and cultural diversity among the student body. As a result of feeling connected, I was more engaged in school, and I turned to research on the effects of pandemic education on students to explain how school connectedness benefits students' well-being.

What I believe to be central to making schools more connected is giving students the opportunity to lead. In my high school, students were active in recognizing diversity among the student body, for example by running cultural clubs and planning multicultural events. Beyond diversity, students also planned assemblies, rallies, and spirit weeks and created chants to cheer on our school at sports games. Overall, I felt like my student body of over three thousand students was connected and enthusiastic—we were unified when it came to competition with our rival schools! I always saw students participate in spirit activities, and these were almost always planned by student clubs with the guidance of their advisers, the school staff. Students know what people in our age group are interested in and have fun doing. And when students lead, they eventually see their contributions in school, feel valued, and encourage those around them to also step up.

My experience with school connectedness has been positive throughout my education, but on a smaller scale, my classrooms are actually not as connected as I'd like them to be. Even though my high school classes were much smaller than the entire student population—thirty-seven students versus three thousand students—there were times when I felt like I didn't have a relationship with my classmates or belong in the same class as them. It's even harder in college—lectures are one, two, three hundred students! I've been taught that the classroom is a place for us to get things done, which is true, but the constant emphasis on work, work, and work has made me put connections on the back burner. I honestly didn't put the effort into engaging with my high school classmates on a personal level because we were inundated with endless assignments and needed to focus on getting through the curriculum before the semester ended.

Now that I'm in college, I've learned to value authentic relationships in the classroom because my peers come from everywhere in the world and have unique ideas that I can learn from. I wish my K–12 classrooms were more connected because I'm sure I would've grown more by learning alongside my peers than from being 100 percent focused on the curriculum. That said, there were some activities my teachers engaged in to foster a classroom culture that I think were successful and should've been done more often across all my classes.

1. THE CLASS WORKS TOGETHER TO ACHIEVE A SHARED GOAL.

Back in elementary school, my teachers often set goals for everyone in the class to meet together. For example, if everyone read a certain number of books by the end of the school year, we were rewarded with an ice cream or pizza party. Junk food is the perfect reward for kids, so all of us did what we could to get there. Elementary school was a long time ago for me, but I remember feeling satisfied when I finally got my ice cream, which wouldn't have happened if it wasn't for the rest of my classmates and their hard work.

As I got older, my teachers didn't do class-wide goal setting anymore. The only time we kind of did was when a teacher went over the statewide standards we were expected to meet by the end of the year, which wasn't much fun or engaging. But there were a few times my high school teachers did help us set a class-wide goal and make me feel more connected with my classmates. In my AP Calculus class, our class goal was for everyone to pass the AP exam by scoring a 3 or higher. I took AP Calculus during my senior year of high school during the COVID-19 pandemic, and I chose to do it 100 percent online but still managed to feel connected with my peers because of this high-pressure goal. Knowing how difficult this class was and how my classmates were also studying hard like me made me feel like we were bonding over one of the hardest academic moments of our lives.

Goal setting in my AP English Language class looked a little different. We didn't exactly have a goal to meet together—we instead had a question to formulate and answer together. When we first started reading a book as a class, every table had to come up with a few questions about the book and make sure they related to rhetoric. Then we shared our questions and voted on the question we wanted to answer as a class as we continued to read the rest of the book. While coming up with a class question isn't exactly the same as my elementary school teachers' reading goals, it's still a collaborative experience where everyone's contributions are acknowledged. Encouraging your students to help set a goal that the class can work toward is a way to get everyone into a "we're in this together" or teamwork mentality.

2. THE CLASS REGULARLY DOES BONDING ACTIVITIES.

The beginning of the school year is when most social activities take place in class to help teachers and students get to know each other. However, I don't think bonding activities should be limited to just the first two weeks of school. As time passes, teachers and students get closer, but it doesn't hurt to regularly spend some of the class period strengthening relationships instead of grinding through the next chapter of content. Doing a class bonding activity brings humanity and empathy into the classroom because we take the time to view our teachers and peers as humans.

When school was remote because of COVID-19, something I looked forward to in one of my classes was Zoom bingo, which we tried to do every month. Everyone turned their cameras on and we responded to a question about our interests, hobbies, or plans with a drawing. Then we shared our drawings and tried to find a row, column, or diagonal of students on the Zoom screen who had the same answer. Zoom bingo was a short activity that helped my classmates and me connect by learning that we had similar interests. It also helped us de-stress because we didn't have anything else on our minds. Class bonding activities don't have to be extravagant and should aim to bring everyone in the classroom together.

Similarly, I did an internship virtually during the summer of my second year of college. My internship program formed peer groups, and each week we met up to play games, learn about each other's projects, and talk about the weekend. I also went to intern meetings outside of my own peer group, and I always had a great experience. These bonding activities created a work environment that was healthy, engaging, and fun, which I think is important because we worked on many large projects that could get stressful. Having the time to get to know each other and chat helped us slow down and not become burned out because the internship wasn't all about working nonstop.

3. STUDENTS' INTERESTS ARE CONNECTED WITH THE CURRICULUM.

This helps create a classroom where students from different backgrounds are welcome and feel like they belong.[13] In my eighth-grade English class, I read *Inside Out and Back Again* by Vietnamese American author Thanhhà Lai. In my AP English Language class, I read *Catfish and Mandala* by Vietnamese American author Andrew X. Pham. Many of the students in both of those classes were also Vietnamese, and we talked about how we felt seen in these books because much of the literature we're taught in school is from the American literary canon, which lacks diverse voices. It was a valuable and empowering experience to see ourselves in our curriculum. I also believe reading texts about diverse experiences is a great way for us to learn more about the people around us, about how we're different and similar. It reminds us that the classroom is full of humans who have experiences to share.

FROM THE TEACHER'S DESK: JENNIFER

Much of what Karen shared about her identity resonates with me. I, too, am a first-generation Canadian, my parents both having been born in Italy. In our conversations while coauthoring this book, I was amazed that despite the huge age gap, her experiences as a child of first-generation immigrants were so incredibly similar to mine. Parent expectations are intense and school is a priority. I also always felt included, culturally speaking, because there were many, many Italian Canadians who attended my school, and let's face it, I'm white. So, although I occasionally got made fun of for my smelly lunch (my parents packed me mortadella sandwiches, which really do smell, while some kids taunted me for eating horse meat), I never really had to deal with microaggressions as a student, either. I was, however, very much alone throughout my elementary and middle-school years. This was because I wore very thick glasses and I had crossed eyes. I often wondered how my school experiences would have been different if I was not always perceived as "other." Thus, when I became a teacher, I was much more in tune with the kids who were ostracized. The problem is that in my early years of teaching, I prioritized content over connection and so I don't think I was necessarily successful in supporting those kids in front of me who may have been struggling with fitting in as much as I would have liked. This is definitely something that resonated with me from Karen's account: work was the priority and other than at the beginning of the year, we didn't have time for bonding.

I watched my students struggle and also felt the impact of disconnectedness and isolation during the pandemic, and with it the realization that check-in activities, music playlists, using pop culture, and making time for getting-to-know-you activities can and should be a regular happening.

Rita Pierson reminds us that kids don't learn from people they don't like, but honestly, when you have SO MUCH content to get through, making connections a priority does not always seem feasible. The following are a few examples from my own practice that have helped me to foster positive connections within my classes and in my school.

CELEBRATING DIFFERENCES

Karen shared in this chapter how impactful it was for her to feel seen and understood because she was able to read texts by Vietnamese authors. She says, "It reminds us that the classroom is full of humans who have experiences to share." Without knowing it, Karen is reinforcing the ideas shared by Rudine Sims Bishop in the article "Mirrors, Windows, and Sliding Glass Doors":

> Books are sometimes windows, offering views of worlds that may be real or imagined, familiar or strange. These windows are also sliding glass doors, and readers have only to walk through in imagination to become part of whatever world has been created and recreated by the author. When lighting conditions are just right, however, a window can also

be a mirror. Literature transforms human experience and reflects it back to us, and in that reflection we can see our own lives and experiences as part of the larger human experience. Reading, then, becomes a means of self-affirmation, and readers often seek their mirrors in books.[14]

It was powerful for Karen and her fellow Vietnamese American classmates to see themselves within the pages of a book, thus affirming their own cultural beliefs, social values, and self-worth. Karen's classmates who are not Vietnamese Canadian may have a new appreciation of differences and similarities with their own experiences and culture and perhaps a change of attitudes and stereotypes. Whether in our own classrooms, or in my case, the school library collection, I am ever mindful of providing my students with opportunities to read texts through which they can see their own experiences or culture.

I consider what Justine Abigail Yu, a guest speaker at our school, shared: "Diversity is not about what makes us different, it's about celebrating what we each bring to our community." So in addition to providing texts that act as mirrors, windows, and sliding glass doors, I have thought a lot about how we might celebrate the contributions students make to our community in order to foster belonging.

Our student council sent a survey to every student in our school to ask about the culture with which they identify. From that information, I added books to our library collection, but we also created a Google Earth project highlighting each country and inviting students to use the tools in Google Earth to look around and learn more about each country.[15] It took us a few hours to add all the cities, but now that it is done, the Google Earth project is one that is shared and updated yearly. We have also asked for music and food contributions, which we share during various times in the year in addition to authors from those countries so I can purchase books that students can see themselves in. As a result of the Google form, we now know the cultural makeup of our school, and so I enlisted our talented Visual Arts Council to create a mural for our library (which I would recommend for the front of the school) with "Welcome" in each language. We specifically decided to paint them on separate speech bubbles so we can continue to add on every year. We also added a physical map. We bought a huge one and invited students to place a dot on the place they would consider to be their heritage. This map is displayed in our library and the kids look at it, comment on it, or ask me about it almost weekly.

Welcome Wall

Most recently, we held a Culture Night which went beyond a tokenistic attempt to learn about culture. We invited students to showcase their culture by submitting a proposal and agreeing to be a "culture captain." The expectation was that the culture captain would have a strong family connection to the culture and would oversee the process. Teams could consist of up to eight students per country, with a teacher supervisor for support. Student teams were given a three-panel bristol board with the following guidelines:

Mandatory elements

- name of country
- general information about the country
- flag
- map indicating location
- the following words in language of the country: "Hello," "Welcome," "I love you," "Thank you"
- two to three songs submitted to committee for a playlist to be played on the evening of the event
- two to three fun facts to be used on the evening of the event
- food samplings with ingredient list for up to two hundred people

Optional elements

- historical timeline(s)
- celebrities, authors, and singers from your country
- submit a performance for the main stage

Students were invited to bring artifacts from their country and dress in clothing typical of their country as well.

Because it was our first time running the event, we honestly didn't have high expectations. We were hoping to get about ten countries and perhaps a hundred participants. We had no real expectation that any students would dress in the costumes of their heritage. We certainly underestimated the impact of this event and the joy and pride with which the culture captains would participate. Grandparents and parents got involved in cooking traditional food, kids came in cultural dress, and there were over 250 people in attendance. We also had singers, dancers, and an accordion player for our main stage presentations. The feedback by everyone in attendance was unanimously positive and I know that this event will only get bigger in the years to come. It was an opportunity to learn more about each other, and the intergenerational collaboration was a wonderful bonus.

LEADERSHIP AND MENTORSHIP: AN AWAY CAMP

We have a unique tradition at my former school. In the first week of school, our ninth graders go to an overnight camp where they engage in community-building activities led exclusively by our eleventh- and twelfth-grade leaders. The organizing teachers do an incredible job of ensuring that the ninth-grade students meet and connect with as many different kids as possible during the trip. Students are placed in a bus grouping, an activity grouping, a table grouping, and a cabin grouping. Each group has approximately twenty ninth graders and four leaders/mentors. Students are also further connected by a color: team green, team red, team purple, and team blue. Kids engage in trust activities, take risks like zip lining and rock-climbing, and complete team challenges and activities. Some of these include using objects in nature to spell out your color, doing the mannequin challenge, creating a team cheer, etc. Points are awarded to groups based on the challenges they complete, as well as kindness, motivating others, trying something new, and encouraging others. It's an incredible three days away. Only it's not. When we come back to school, the ninth graders recognize one another and more importantly, the twelfth graders look out for their ninth-grade buddies. Many stay connected even after students graduate. The organizing team spends a great deal of time helping senior kids recognize their leadership potential, and the experience is one that kids reflect on as the best part of their entire high school experience. It is truly magical. Our administrator not only supported the initiative but would also come to camp to spend time connecting with kids and engaging in activities. I would invite teachers to see if there is an opportunity to partner with an overnight camp in their area to bring this experience to your school.

THE POWER OF MUSIC

If there is one thing that in my experience kids prioritize, it's the impact of music in their lives. Noa Daniel, a teacher in Ontario, shares about her Personal Playlist Project in her TEDx Kitchener talk.[16] People are asked to share three songs: one that is nostalgic, one that reflects their identity, and a song that is their favorite pick-me-up. Daniel invited me on her podcast, and the experience of selecting these three songs was so powerful that I brought it into the classroom.

Initially, students created a "Bitmoji" room that featured their "identity song." They were placed in groups and shared why the song they chose was reflective of their identity. Later in the year, I asked students for their favorite "pick-me-up" song and used the song titles to create a Spotify playlist. Whenever we had a work period, I would play this playlist; seeing kids light up because their song was playing was magical. Several of my students shared how much they loved that they were able to contribute a song to the playlist. I think asking kids for their nostalgic song from elementary school would be an awesome thing to implement for twelfth graders!

Connecting songs to poetry and having kids connect a song to a concept or book they are studying are other ways to bring in music in meaningful ways that complement our curriculum. Some books now come with Spotify playlists, and many people on #BookTok share their playlists with books. I have brought this into our school's book club, which has taught me more about my students not just because of the songs they select, but because of what resonates for them based on the passages they select for the songs.

ESCAPE ROOM GAMES OR BREAKOUT EDU IN THE CLASSROOM

Karen suggests in this chapter that being 100 percent focused on the curriculum is not as important as learning alongside her peers. Her student perspective is that learning alongside her peers is mutually exclusive from uncovering the curriculum. I find this fascinating, and I wonder about the extent to which she may have collaborative learning experiences around curriculum expectations but does not think of them as such. In my experience, we can do both: we can help kids uncover curriculum expectations while allowing them to engage in fun and collaborative experiences with a shared goal. This is why I am such a fan of escape room games and Breakout EDU. Going to escape rooms has become a tradition in my family. If you are unfamiliar with the concept, it goes like this: you are put in a room and given a certain amount of time to unlock puzzles and solve riddles in order to "escape." We once went to Casa Loma, a local castle here in Toronto, Ontario, and collaborated with eighteen people to escape a 1920s Prohibition-themed game.

Breakout EDU is an educational platform that makes it easy! Breakout EDU has games around every subject area and grade (some of them FREE) that you can pick up and use if you have their breakout boxes (although lots of educators make up their own boxes from locks purchased on Amazon). I have cocreated games with teachers around math and science concepts, Shakespearean plays, and a fingerprinting forensics game for a law class. Playing the games can be a fun way to foster connections and teamwork among students as well as a way to unpack content, and the ideal is to have kids create mini-games for each other to build valuable critical thinking skills.

At my former school, a group of student leaders created escape room–style activities for younger students around anti-vaping through our OSAID (Ontario Students Against Impaired Driving) Council. They traveled to local middle schools to have students play the games. The result was an amazing leadership and learning experience for everyone involved!

MAKE SOCIAL EMOTIONAL LEARNING (SEL) A PRIORITY, NOT AN AFTERTHOUGHT

Casel.org defines social emotional learning as "the process through which children and adults understand and manage emotions, set and achieve positive goals, feel and show empathy for others, establish and maintain positive relationships, and make responsible decisions." For many years, we looked at these as "soft skills" that were not necessary to a student's academic success. Throughout the pandemic, there was a shift as we realized that social emotional learning might be more important than we thought. Today, many of my featured talks and keynote requests are centered around social emotional learning and digital life. This may be because we have come to realize, as Dr. Katie Martin states in *Evolving Education: Shifting to a Learner-Centered Paradigm*, that relationships and SEL in learner-centered environments are "the foundation of effective learning communities."[17]

Research supports the effectiveness of SEL as well. According to a landmark meta-analysis involving more than 270,000 students, results showed the following:

- SEL interventions that address the five core competencies increased students' academic performance by 11 percentile points, compared to students who did not participate.
- Students participating in SEL programs showed improved classroom behavior, an increased ability to manage stress and depression, and better attitudes about themselves, others, and school.[18]

CASEL, one of the leading resources around social emotional learning, identifies a framework with the following subset of skills:

- Self-awareness: the abilities to understand one's emotions, thought, and values and how they influence behavior across contexts

- Self-management: the abilities to manage one's emotions, thoughts, and behaviors effectively in different situations to achieve goals and aspirations
- Responsible decision-making: the abilities to make caring and constructive choices about personal behavior and social interactions across diverse situations
- Relationship skills: the abilities to establish and maintain healthy and supportive relationships and to effectively navigate settings with diverse individuals and groups
- Social awareness: the abilities to understand the perspectives of and empathize with others, including those from diverse backgrounds, cultures, and contexts.[19]

Because we have so much on our plates, it is sometimes daunting to think about how we might explicitly tackle all of these skills, but just knowing what they are and that they are important can often help me decide which activities support which skill. Whenever possible, I choose activities that I know will help students develop several of them at once.

A focus on **mental health and digital wellness** can take several forms and helps students with self-management and self-awareness. Although many would argue that getting rid of technology altogether would be ideal, there are several ideas that utilize technology. There are a variety of resources online that offer nature and animal cams that can transport your classroom to a place far from stress. You can visit the Seattle Aquarium, watch elephants at a watering hole in South Africa, or watch an eagle's nest. Asking kids how they feel when they are watching the animals versus how they feel when they spend a great deal of time on a screen is an important reflection question. With older students, we talk explicitly about cell-phone management. Since we know that our phones are designed to grab our attention, having students share the strategies they use to ensure they stay focused on tasks will help students hone this skill.

One-minute sharing can provide a way to support several SEL skills including self-awareness and relationship skills. During the pandemic, when we were all virtual, I used meme check-ins, an idea shared by Jenn Giffen. I invited students to have a look at several images and decide which one was closest to how they were feeling. For younger students, it can be a great vocabulary-building tool as well.[20]

How are you feeling today?

When we went back to in-person learning, I abandoned these check-ins. Back to "normal," I rationalized. And yet, a one-minute check-in in the form of these memes had helped us to connect with each other, and I felt that to be missing, so I immediately brought them back. Other one-minute sharing prompts that help kids develop stronger relationships with one another and have helped strengthen their connections are as follows:

- "Would you rather" prompts.
- Share a smile or frown from the week.
- Share one thing you are grateful for.
- Share one thing you learned outside of school this week.
- Share one song that is stuck in your head.

I always ask kids to share with a partner first, set a timer for one minute, and then invite whole-class sharing. This is so every student has a voice. Admittedly when all is said and done, this takes closer to five minutes, but the results have been worth it, and I always learn something new about at least one of my students.

A FOCUS ON EMPATHY

Karen shares that "doing a class bonding activity brings humanity and empathy into the classroom because we take the time to view our teachers and peers as humans." Building empathy, according to CASEL, falls within social awareness, and I would argue it is one of the most important skills we can help our students develop. In my book *Social LEADia: Moving Students from Digital Citizenship to Digital Leadership*, I talk about how much of an impact connecting with other classes around the world has had on my students. I leverage my own social media connections to find people, organizations, or classrooms with whom to connect with literally a click of a button. One of the most powerful connections I share in the book is the connection we had with an indigenous community four hours away in distance but culturally a thousand miles away. That connection helped my students see beyond stereotypes to the human teens who were just like them.

Another way I help kids build empathy is to have them look at a post, article, or issue from a variety of perspectives. Julie Millan shared this idea she used with third-grade students with me, and I have used it with success in my high school classrooms when I am trying to help students understand their biases.[21] The reason it works so effectively is that it helps kids understand the extent to which their own experiences impact the way they see the world. Here's a simple example:

The school board cancels the buses because of poor weather conditions. Students in groups share their opinion based on their role:

- Green hat: You are the school board who made this decision.

- Yellow hat: You are a parent who has an important presentation at work and now don't know what to do about your kids not being able to get to school.
- White hat: You are a school bus driver
- Blue hat: You are a student who takes the bus to school.

Students struggle responding in their roles and trying on different perspectives, but they get better at it as we ask them to practice. It is important for our students to understand that whomever they encounter, whether in person or online, will have a different opinion, but seeing a variety of points of view will help us become more empathetic.

Casel.org offers so many comprehensive resources to help you on your journey to making SEL a more intentional part of your classroom.

IDEA SPOTLIGHT
ENGAGE IN THE ONGOING JOURNEY OF DISCOVERING WHO OUR STUDENTS ARE

When we think about getting to know our students, it includes what they like and don't like, what they do and don't do, but it should also include the *why* behind those interests and actions. To truly get to know our students and the stories and experiences that make them who they are, we need to recognize the layers and intersections of their identities. Some of our identities like race, gender, or religion may be visible through a person's skin tone, facial features, or clothing; however, we need to recognize that it is an incomplete story. How two or more identities (race and gender) interact makes it more challenging to understand how a student moves through life. We often rely on stereotypes, make assumptions, or believe what someone has told us about that student to fill in the gaps, tricking ourselves that we truly know who this person is. We must acknowledge that building relationships takes time, persistence, and effort as we are attempting to be stewards of a young person's personal information. And as they experience life, make mistakes, and celebrate victories, who they are from when you first meet them will evolve and change. Getting to know our students is not a one-time event but a recurring one.

When trying to make learning relevant to our students, we sometimes rely on our versions of who we think our students are. By doing this, we sometimes deliver a lesson that misses the mark. When trying to make learning more relevant, educators may start to include days of significance in their learning spaces. However, when we assume that a student celebrates a specific day of significance based on who we think they are, this can be hurtful despite our good intentions. When this happens, it is important to not dismiss it. One approach is to think of the four As: apologize, acknowledge, address, and adjust. Apologizing for the negative impact and acknowledging it with the impacted student is important to start a dialogue. Addressing it with all the learners and sharing how you will adjust the lesson/activities helps to build trust in your community of learners.

JASON TRINH, COORDINATOR, GLOBAL COMPETENCIES,
STEM/ICT DISTRICT COORDINATOR, DIGITAL LEARNING

IDEA SPOTLIGHT
DEVELOPING AUTHENTIC RELATIONSHIPS WITH STUDENTS

> "Every child deserves a champion, an adult who will never give up on them, who understands the power of connection, and insists that they become the best that they can possibly be."
>
> — RITA PIERSON

Perhaps the most important thing we can do as educators is focus on our students as human beings versus human doings. There are so many components of schooling that require students to do, to perform, to master, to apply, and to analyze. However, over the past two years the world has gotten an intimate front-row seat to the power of developing authentic relationships with students in a way that transcends simply the doing. Teacher leaders, schools leaders, and district leaders are beginning to understand how critical it is that we embrace our students as human beings—human beings with thoughts, feelings, experiences, and perspectives that when leveraged and supported appropriately creates monumental transformation in our students' lives and in schools.

What would happen to the world of education as we know it if every educational stakeholder committed to developing simply one transparent and authentic relationship with a child in their educational community? What would happen to the future of our country if every child who attended an institution of teaching and learning had a fierce advocate that championed their success and provided their undivided attention to ensure that child had the resources and support necessary to accomplish their goals and dreams?

One of the best ways to develop authentic relationships with students is to meet one on one with each child in your classroom at least once a quarter/report period. During this protected time, focus the conversations on the student's celebrations and challenges in order to gain insight into that particular student's world. When educators truly "see" their students, it opens up opportunities to make critical shifts in our thinking and approach to teaching and learning.

As the late Rita Pierson mentioned, we would begin to see a world full of competent, confident, and charismatic leaders, speakers, and thinkers who paid it forward. The power of building relationships with students is a uniquely rare opportunity to influence the

HOPES FOR SCHOOL

twenty-second century. As twenty-first century leaders, we cannot afford not to.

DR. MARY HEMPHILL, CEO AND FOUNDER OF THE LIMITLESS LEADER LLC AND SENIOR FELLOW AT THE CENTER FOR MODEL SCHOOLS

DISCUSSION QUESTIONS

1. How might you learn more about the diversity of your students?
2. What is one thing that you already do to build a sense of belonging or community?
3. How do you balance curriculum and connection?
4. What is one idea from this chapter that resonates?

CHAPTER 4
HOMEWORK

FROM THE STUDENT'S DESK: KAREN

I quit playing field hockey twice in high school. The first time was the summer of my sophomore year right after tryouts, around when I started taking community college classes through concurrent enrollment. I wanted to get more college credit on top of taking AP classes and exams. Field hockey was a massive time commitment during the summer and the fall (sometimes we had to travel to Los Angeles for games, and we'd get back to Orange County at 8:00 p.m.). I was terrified that I would do poorly in my classes, especially my community college ones because they're designed for college students, so I quit to make more time for school. I ended up hating PE so much that I rejoined the team, but I had to work extra hard to keep my grades up. I wasn't the only one who suffered during the season. When we had games, it was common for us to do our homework on the bus or on the grass under the hot sun while we waited for the varsity team to finish their match. Even after starting school at 8:00 a.m. and having a long game day, we were still students when we got home if we didn't finish our homework or study enough yet.

The second time I quit (*really quit*) was the summer of my junior year. I was taking three AP classes as a junior (English, biology, and United States history), and I had to worry about volunteering and clubs because junior year is arguably the most important year of high school if you want to go to college. If I had continued to play field hockey, I most definitely would've lost my mind because I had a ridiculous amount of homework that year on top of other commitments: I became an editor for my student newspaper, volunteered on Saturday mornings, and had Vietnamese language classes on Sunday mornings.

While I don't miss sweating buckets under the sun and getting hit by hard plastic balls, I will say quitting field hockey was hard both times. The sport is challenging, and my teammates were funny and I liked spending time with them (and I was in the best shape of my life—I wasn't nearly as active after I quit). A lot of students pick up sports so they can add "varsity letterman" to their college applications, but field hockey was one of two activities I did for my own enrichment and not for school—the other was being part of my student newspaper.

I've been hearing more and more about work-life balance since I started working in college: you need to set boundaries at work so you don't bring work into your home and personal life. Otherwise, you're going to be miserable and not have a personal life at all because everything is about work, work, work. The thing is, students don't have the luxury of setting such boundaries and separating our school and personal lives. We have no work-life balance. We *have* to bring our work home—it's called "homework" for a reason. Not only that, but so many of the activities we do outside of school like athletics or volunteering for clubs are still for school, college applications, and scholarships.

BEING A STUDENT FROM 7:00 A.M. TO MIDNIGHT

One of my favorite articles on education is "Burnt Out on the High School Treadmill" by Candy Schulman, which was published as an opinion piece by the *Washington Post* in 2011. Schulman details the growing stress her sixteen-year-old daughter experiences as a junior in high school:

> She knows that everyone feels pressure to get through six tests in one week plus a complex paper and hours of

homework each night. Others are also touring colleges on weekends even though they can't really spare time away from studying, participating in sports, practicing an instrument, fulfilling community service requirements, or rising to leadership positions to put on college résumés. And oh, yes, how about showing colleges you have a job, too?[1]

My middle-school self couldn't have imagined having this exact experience in high school. I used to think it was ridiculous that people stayed up past 10:00 p.m. to do their homework because our assignments were easy: readings, short worksheets, textbook problems, and the occasional essay. I swore I'd never be like that because I always had good time management skills and work ethic. I did my homework the second I got home, and sometimes I could even finish it while I was at school. I soon sadly discovered that high school was an entirely different beast that demanded so much of me. As Schulman wrote, being a student isn't just being enrolled in an educational institution, going to classes, and calling it a day once the last bell of the day has rung. Even though my first class started at 7:10 a.m. and my school day ended at 1:30 p.m., I was still a student until I did all of my school-related activities and homework, and I usually went to sleep at or after midnight.

I believe that as time passed, I began to burn out on the high school treadmill like Schulman's daughter did. I had excellent grades, but it took me longer than usual to get work done. My days began to look like this: getting home from school, starting my first assignment, and constantly zoning out so it took me too long to get things done. Any free time I had to myself was usually spent napping or doing absolutely nothing. I was too tired to entertain any of my hobbies; I don't even think I had hobbies, and I only hung out with friends during school breaks because my life revolved around school from September to June. Actually, I was still doing school over the summer because I had summer assignments. In the summer of my junior year of high school, I had to study for the SAT exam. I also decided to take the ACT, which led to even more studying while I was in school. My extracurriculars took up a lot of time and energy, but homework drained me the most.

The value and necessity of homework have long been discussed, and there's plenty of research that supports the many perspectives in this debate. I know there is contradictory research on the value of homework, but as a student, I'm not as interested in that as I am in sharing my own personal experiences: what my homework was like, the toll homework took on me, and what other students are saying about homework. To be clear, I'm not advocating to eliminate all homework, because it can be helpful.

In my English, Spanish, and history/social studies classes, I usually had reading and writing assignments to do. My science homework was the same, but sometimes I'd have to do pre-lab preparation and worksheets and watch videos. Almost all of my math homework was doing problems from the textbook. It was also common for there to be group projects in most of my classes, which required meeting and working outside of class time. At first glance, that seems like reasonable homework for each class, and I agree that it is. Many of my homework assignments were straightforward, related to the material in class, and predictable (e.g., I wasn't doing practice problems for my English classes and reading novels for my math classes).

The thing is, I had *all* of those homework assignments to do almost *every day* in high school. If my homework assignments weren't mandatory and didn't affect my grade, I would've chosen to not complete most of them because I either didn't need the extra practice or didn't see how the work was beneficial (for example, I can't understand the purpose of a word search and what skill or knowledge I am supposed to get from completing it). In a voluntary survey I conducted in high school for this book, twenty-one students out of thirty-two respondents had similar answers to this question: "What is one thing teachers do that INHIBITS your learning and makes you not want to learn/hate school?" Most students who responded took AP/honors courses.

These twenty-one students said that (excessive) homework, repetitive and pointless homework, and busywork made them hate school. One student, Remi, responded by saying, "While I understand that homework is necessary to retain information, there should be a limit, too. Taking multiple rigorous courses with a heavy workload will only add to the student's stress." Another student, Avery, said, "We become swamped with homework and have no time to enjoy our youth."

It's not just students at my high school who feel this way. *Three Penny Press*, the student newspaper from Bellaire High School in Bellaire, Texas, reported in January 2022 that its students spend three times longer on homework than the average found in a 2018–2020 survey conducted by Challenge Success.[2] According to this Challenge Success survey, which included over fifty thousand high schoolers over a two-year period, students reported doing an average of 2.7 hours of work per day on weekdays. *Three Penny Press* surveyed approximately two hundred of its students, and this is what they found: 43 percent spent three to five hours per day on homework, 14 percent spent six to eight hours, and 5 percent spent nine hours. In addition, 77 percent of respondents said a healthy number of homework hours is zero to two hours per day.[3]

I acknowledge that my teachers tried their best to keep their homework assignments reasonable in terms of difficulty and time to complete (anywhere from fifteen minutes to one hour). But students have homework for multiple classes every day—it adds up to us spending hours on homework. The workload in AP courses is far worse, and my peers and I usually took multiple honors/AP courses each year. I can imagine that the work in nonaccelerated classes is more demanding now than it was ten years ago, too. Some days were good and I only had a total of two short assignments to do, but (most) other days I had difficult math homework, an essay to write, textbook problems for chemistry, and an exam to study for. There were days when I spent five hours on homework, which is more time than I spent on my extracurriculars. For example, field hockey practice during the fall season (when we have games and competitions) lasted around three hours. A typical high school week for me looked like this: I'm at school for almost eight hours Monday through Friday, then I have three hours of sports practice, and then I could have up to five hours' worth of homework to do. Being a student is exhausting.

While we're on the topic of homework, I also want to point out that there is research proving the benefits of homework and advocates for homework often say "quality" homework is what's making a difference and helping students succeed academically. Developmental psychologist Janine Bempechat wrote in her 2019 article "The Case for (Quality) Homework" that students should receive "high-quality, challenging assignments—and it is this kind of homework that has been associated with higher achievement." Bempechat defines high-quality homework as homework that is "developmentally appropriate and meaningful," "promote[s] self-regulation," is "authentic, allowing students to engage with real-world relevance," and "make[s] efficient use of student time and [has] a clear purpose connected to what they [students] are learning."[4] Susan Brookhart, a professor emerita of education at Duquesne University, believes that quality assignments lead to quality feedback. As we discussed in chapter 1, feedback is important, especially when students learn how they can improve in the future. Brookhart writes in the second edition of her book *How to Give Effective Feedback to Your Students* that assignments should be aligned with explicit learning targets (i.e., require students to use relevant knowledge, skills, and cognitive processes).[5] There should also be clear expectations and directions.

Toward the end of this chapter, I'll talk more about what "quality" homework looks like to me, but for now, I have to say that I believe there's no point in assigning your students quality homework if they're being inundated with a massive load of homework every day. One student responded to my survey, saying, "When [homework] gets to be too much, it changes my perspective and makes me want to slack rather than do my best." I feel the same way. On days when I have a lot of homework to do, I don't care about the assignment, the intention, and doing my best on it. I'll take as many shortcuts as I can, meaning I'm not benefiting from doing the work. I'm not proud of doing that because it means I may end up having a poor foundation, but it doesn't matter. I just want to get it done as soon as possible and get enough points for a good grade because I have other assignments and things going on in my life that I also need to get through with what little time I have.

AN INTERLUDE: I HATE ONLINE LEARNING MANAGEMENT SYSTEMS

During my summers in college, I do full-time internships. I get a work laptop from the company, and once the work day ends, I log off, close my laptop, and don't hear or think about work until the next day.

If only I could do that with my school's learning management system (LMS). I know that using an LMS has benefits that have made educators' and students' lives easier, but I dislike LMSs. In fact, I would say I hate them. My issue with LMSs is that they extend the school day into my personal life and remind me of school at inappropriate hours, which I consider being between 5:00 p.m. to 6:00 a.m.

I didn't start using an online LMS until middle school. Things were suddenly due at 11:59 p.m. Some students might prefer having this late deadline, but I'd rather have work due before our next class. This would give me more flexibility in how I structure my time. For example, instead of being reminded that I should worry about school at 11:59 p.m., I'd already be in bed, knowing I could wake up a little earlier to finish that assignment. (Of course, this makes the most sense for assignments that teachers don't plan to grade first thing in the morning.)

Even if the 11:59 p.m. deadline becomes a 5:00 p.m. deadline, it's not like we can stop worrying about school. We have our LMS notifications on to be alerted of any important announcements made at any time of the day. We also keep them on so we know when grades are released. There's nothing better than learning you got a bad score on a test at 7:00 p.m. while you're eating dinner or getting assignment notifications over the weekend (yes, we're still students on weekends because we have weekend homework). Online LMSs never free us from school.

WHAT WORKS FOR ME

As I mentioned earlier in this chapter, I don't think teachers should stop assigning homework altogether. I benefit from doing math homework because it helps me develop my terrible math knowledge and skills, and if my English teachers never asked us to read our books before coming to class, it would take us months to finish analyzing a single book together. However, like the twenty-one students in my survey who condemned repetitive and unhelpful homework, I don't appreciate having assignments like "busywork, which doesn't help you learn, but only sucks away your time," as one student, Hunter, said. We're already in our classes for seven to eight hours a day, equivalent to full-time work hours. It's hard to have a personal life, take care of ourselves, and not be a student for once when everything revolves around school. Students deserve to have their time respected so what we're working on outside of school can be a good use of our time and energy.

1. WHEN MY TEACHERS ARE CLEAR ABOUT THE PURPOSE AND LEARNING OUTCOMES OF OUR HOMEWORK.

As simple as it sounds, having a short objective or purpose statement at the beginning of an assignment helps make it abundantly clear what the teacher's intentions are for this assignment: what students are meant to utilize from class in this practice and how it will prepare them for their exams or projects. When my teachers explained in the homework write-up how this practice would be applied in class in the future, I could understand the relevance of their assignments and tended to take the class more seriously. I've had countless homework assignments that felt so random, like fill-in-the-blank worksheets, word searches, or writing down definitions. Sure, these are short and easy, so they won't take up too much time. What won't take up any time whatsoever, however, is simply not assigning busywork like this because in the end, what value does a word search have in my learning and how will it help me when a midterm exam that's not vocabulary-based comes around?

This isn't something my teachers did, but I would've liked to see them do it: state how long it should take to complete a homework assignment. That really forces you to design work that has value but doesn't take unnecessarily long. English teacher Mary Davenport wrote in her 2020 Edutopia article "Rethinking Homework for This Year—and Beyond" that her school's teachers agreed that homework assignments should take thirty minutes or less to complete. I also agree with that. Your homework assignments should not be putting my entire life on pause. It shouldn't require me to teach myself a bunch of brand-new topics, which certainly takes more than thirty minutes, that weren't covered in class before the bell rang. Davenport added that at her school, the goal is to have students complete as much work in class as possible, and she listens to her students:

> In true partnership with my students, I'm constantly checking in with them via Google Forms, Zoom chats, conferences, and Padlet activities. In these check-ins, I specifically ask students how they're managing the workload for my class and their other classes. I ask them how much homework they're doing. And I adjust what I do and expect based on what they tell me. For example, when I find out a week is heavy with work in other classes, I make sure to allot more time during class for my tasks. At times I have even delayed or altered one of my assignments.[6]

She also includes the maximum time limit on top of her students' assignments, which is such a healthy practice. It shows she's mindful of her students' time. It also helps them plan out their days or weeks knowing how much time they might be doing homework.

2. WHEN MY TEACHERS USE HOMEWORK AS A WAY TO REINFORCE WHAT WE LEARNED.

The second-worst type of homework (the first is busywork) is homework that we forget all about after we turn it in. As I've reiterated over and over again, students are students for most of the day. It's unfair to have us do work that we don't discuss or get feedback on, because we forget all about it. I've had teachers say our homework is useful to review for exams, but that's only true to some extent. The homework doesn't help us if it's busywork, or if it has nothing to do with the exam, or if we get things wrong on the homework and receive no feedback on it. Homework isn't helpful to me if we turn it in and do nothing with it afterward because it feels like everything I was supposed to learn was thrown away. If the homework isn't important enough to discuss in class afterward or receive feedback on, why did we have to do it in the first place?

In addition to making sure homework is utilized in the classroom, I'm also an advocate for allowing students to redo assignments that may be more high-stakes than others. Like we've discussed in chapter 1, giving students second chances is valuable. If homework is meant to reinforce what we've learned, then we should be allowed to apply our knowledge again once we receive feedback.

3. WHEN MY TEACHERS RECORD THEIR LESSONS OR DO FLIPPED CLASSROOMS.

One education-related outcome from the COVID-19 pandemic that I enjoy is recorded lessons. There are educators who've always done this, but it became more common during virtual learning. Even as we transitioned back to in-person learning, I had plenty of teachers who continued to record their lectures. Recording lectures during class and uploading them for students to watch afterward is a helpful practice because students who didn't fully grasp the concepts in class can take a look at the video on their own time. Moreover, it encourages students to be more engaged in class and participate instead of frantically taking notes because they know they can always revisit the lesson afterward.

Similarly, I've had teachers who do flipped classrooms wherein all of the lecture material is delivered via video and we spend class time reviewing the lesson and doing practice activities. I like this practice because, again, the recorded lessons make it easier for me to pace myself. This support mattered a lot in my AP Calculus class because I struggled constantly, especially because of how fast-paced AP courses are. The best thing about delivering instruction through video is that I can pause or rewind parts of the video whenever I need to. It also helps to create an online Q&A forum where students can ask questions whenever they need to since there is limited live instruction.

FROM THE TEACHER'S DESK: JENNIFER

For the last six years, I have taught at an International Baccalaureate (IB) world school for seven years. In one of my previous teaching positions, I taught AP courses, and as I read Karen's words here, I can definitely empathize with students who sent me 4:00 a.m. questions and walked around like zombies because of lack of sleep. As a teacher, the question of homework has always been like balancing on a tightrope for me: when I didn't assign enough, parents would be upset because in their opinion, nothing good could come from a teen with extra time on their hands. When it's too much, then that is problematic as well for the many reasons Karen has stated. To add to the complexity, we have an established "minimum and maximum" homework minutes as part of our board policy that is not unlike the policies of schools around the world. Here is an example:

> *As a general guideline, the daily average number of homework minutes is ten (10) minutes per grade as follows:*

> *Grades 1–3: 10–30 minutes*
> *Grades 4–6: 40–60 minutes*
> *Grades 7–8: 70–80 minutes*
> *Grades 9–12: 90—120 minutes**
>
> **Certain programs of study such as International Baccalaureate (IB) and Advanced Placement (AP) may require daily averages that exceed these guidelines in order to meet curriculum expectations.*

Ten minutes per grade seems very reasonable, and yet 120 daily minutes or more of homework for a high school student after a full day of school is daunting. The other problem with high school is that oftentimes as an English teacher, I don't talk to the science teacher down the hall; early on in my career, I asked students to work on my own subject for 120 minutes a day AND they were getting the same amount from each of their four other subject teachers. The math there is very perplexing. I often wish I could go back and apologize to my early AP classes for the amount of homework I assigned!

HOMEWORK AND EQUITY

More and more, when I looked at the big picture (as a literacy consultant looking back and as a teacher-librarian who co-teaches other people's classes), it is easy to see that homework can in fact be linked to equity. I think of my own experiences as a child. Because my parents could not read or write in English, I never got the same level of help that I was able to offer my own children as a middle class, English-speaking parent. We needed Styrofoam balls, wire, paint, and glue to create the solar system? No problem. Whereas my projects in school looked like a second grader completed them (because I literally did on my own), my kids' second-grade projects looked beautiful because of the amount of help I gave them and the quality of the materials I was able to afford. But I know that my kids' classmates did not have that luxury; their parents were working double shifts and didn't have the same time or funds as I did. As my kids got older, this continued to be the case and became even more problematic. You see, some of my students did not have the time to work on homework because they were working a part-time job (sometimes even more than one) to help support their families at home. It was a lose/lose situation for them because their learning skills and often their grades were impacted by that which they could not control.

During the pandemic, another thing became glaringly clear. When we assign something electronically, on an LMS for example, a child needs a computer, tablet, or Chromebook to complete their work, but in any given household, there may only be one computer for everyone to share. For this reason, I tried to get to know my students' circumstances at home, and often, I really cut back on homework.

FLIPPED CLASSROOM VIDEOS FOR HOMEWORK

I remember cofacilitating a workshop on the flipped classroom in 2016, and here, in 2025, Karen is mentioning a flipped classroom approach as one that worked for her learning. Most of the tools I shared for video creation (with the exception of iMovie) no longer exist, but the pedagogical approach itself stands the test of time. By flipping elements of instruction, the teacher becomes more of a facilitator because the content doesn't need to happen during the time you are together. Instead, that time can be spent working on problems and having learning conversations. When I take important concepts and create short videos for my students, I can't always guarantee that they will come to class having watched the videos. Again, in terms of equity, do they have access to the internet at home, are they stuck at a part-time job? And so the next day, I need a space for students to watch and take notes on the video. For the rest of the students, I put them in groups, with a chart paper or collaborative doc or whiteboard, ready to work on something connected to what they learned at home. For example, if the lesson was on different ways a narrator demonstrates character traits, I give students a character from the book we are studying to brainstorm what we know about the character. If it was a math or science lesson, students can apply the learning to an open question. My role in that time is to go around to groups asking questions and supporting the thinking.

In some ways, the pandemic necessitated greater confidence and competence to create videos to support student learning (at least it did in my school), and so there are a ton of tools for video creation and editing. For example, many teachers (and students) are using TikTok as a way to create short content videos because it's so easy to use. Because TikTok is blocked for many students, I download the videos and put them on my YouTube channel or add them directly to my lessons. The flipped classroom model provides a good way to approach the ever-challenging homework dilemma.

SETTING HEALTHY BOUNDARIES

Karen's "hate" of the LMS was surprising to me; after all, an LMS is designed to support students by providing a repository of resources and work so they have it at their disposal at all times. In truth, it's not the LMS itself but rather not having healthy boundaries that Karen finds problematic. One thing I changed immediately after reading her narrative was due dates. I used to use the default of 11:59 p.m. without really thinking about it, and now, I set due dates to 7:00 or 8:00 p.m. This sends the message that students should not be working past that on a school day. I also make a point of negotiating due dates and times with students so they feel a part of the process. In terms of a constant stream of announcements, I always thought that "chunking information" into separate posts would provide a good way to help kids stay on track. After hearing Karen's opinion, I spoke about this practice with my own daughter and students and they, too, identified that the stream of announcements made them anxious. So now, I make sure to keep these at a minimum so as not to overwhelm students. I use bullets, bold, and underline to emphasize what they need to pay attention to, but I keep announcements to a minimum now unless necessary.

When Karen shared that she felt like a student 24/7 because of homework and the LMS, it made me think of my own work-home balance (or lack thereof). When I assigned homework, I felt like I had to mark it. When students emailed me at 11:00 p.m., I felt compelled to answer. My marking piles got bigger and bigger and my resentment also increased. I would take my marking to family get-togethers, and I would decline invitations to go out with friends because I had homework! Oftentimes, I wouldn't start on anything until I had tucked my own children in bed, which meant I was already exhausted. A few ideas for this problem include the following:

- Setting boundaries for myself. I decided which days of the week I would not bring home work, and I created office hours. I made this transparent to my students by saying that to protect family time, I don't bring home work or respond to emails on Tuesdays, Thursdays, and Saturdays. I thought I would get pushback, but kids just got used to this AND as a bonus, it's a good way to model well-being habits for my students.
- A shift to formative assessment helped me lessen my at-home workload. Rather than taking home everything to mark, I began to set up workshop periods whereby I conferenced with kids about their writing. During this time, I also asked students to workshop one another's work. Although exhausting in class, students got feedback to improve their work without me having to bring home a class set of marking.
- Metacognition. We talked about this before in terms of grading. The bonus of helping kids to evaluate their own learning and set goals means that you have marks you can enter for reporting, without having done the heavy lifting.

ANOTHER IDEA: USE AI TO EVALUATE HOMEWORK RESPONSES

When a new tool called ChatGPT hit the internet, there was an uproar. Why assign homework if a student could just put a prompt into the ChatGPT box and a response would be autogenerated? Exactly. But what if, as teachers, we embraced the capabilities and flipped the switch. Ben Thompson, author of *Stratechery*, wrote an article called "AI Homework" that shared the example of his daughter, who was looking to find out more about "The Trial of Napoleon" for her European history class and asked for help understanding the role of Thomas Hobbes, witness for the defense. When Thompson put the question to ChatGPT, the response was incorrect. This is unusual, as typical responses are mostly accurate, but it invites the question of how we might embrace the reality of tools such as ChatGPT to replace homework questions while helping students to think critically about the use of AI in their learning. This might look like this:

1. At the beginning of class, write a "homework question" on the board.
2. Invite students to brainstorm questions to ask ChatGPT (or whatever AI bot is popular when you are reading this book).
3. With a partner, ask students to evaluate how well the bot responded and identify how the answer could be improved.

It is important to note here that, at the time of writing, AI tools are not appropriate for kids under eighteen without parent permission, so as we think creatively about how we can shift homework conversations using AI, we need to think about terms of use, ethics, and reliability as well.

IDEA SPOTLIGHT
DITCH THAT HOMEWORK

When I was teaching high school Spanish, I ditched my homework. I just quit assigning it. After years of ineffective assignments, arguments, and excuses, I decided that it wasn't worth the trouble anymore. I also considered the arguments it caused at home, the lack of conclusive research on its effectiveness, and the uneven playing field it created for my most marginalized students. After that, there was no going back.

Veteran math teacher Alice Keeler agreed with me—so much so that we coauthored a book called *Ditch That Homework* with our best suggestions and practices for replacing homework with what works better.

So... what works better? What can help us reduce our reliance on homework so much that we can reduce it—or completely ditch it?

One of my best and favorite suggestions is to optimize your instructional time (and there are lots of ways to do that). Time in the classroom is precious. Students have access to their highly qualified teacher in the classroom. Distractions are minimized. Everyone has access to the same resources. Plus, we know who's completing the work (which we don't when we assign homework to be done outside of class).

Here are some of my favorite practices to optimize instructional time as tightly as possible, making the most of it:

- **Use retrieval practice.** When students recall information from their brains—rather than look it up in notes or a book—it strengthens long-term memory. Use it frequently as a study strategy (rather than a graded assessment).
- **Provide lots of feedback.** The late Grant Wiggins, an education thought leader, wrote, "Research shows that less teaching plus more feedback is the key to achieving greater learning." Timely, personalized feedback is powerful. And

HOPES FOR SCHOOL

feedback doesn't have to be provided by the teacher. Auto-graded quizzes show students whether answers are right or wrong. Plus, peer feedback can be valuable.

- **Create meaningful repetitions.** Practice makes proficient. Get students meaningful reps on key content, especially baseline, foundational content. It's like pouring a concrete foundation for a building. When they have those core understandings in place, you can build something amazing on that firm foundation.[7]

MATT MILLER, EDUCATOR, SPEAKER,
AUTHOR OF *DITCH THAT TEXTBOOK*

IDEA SPOTLIGHT
THE HOMEWORK MENU: ENHANCING STUDENT VOICE AND CHOICE AT HOME

As a fourth-grade teacher, I was required to assign daily homework but didn't understand why. The students who needed the extra practice tended to be the ones least likely to do it, while the students who didn't need the practice were the ones who did it anyway. So why was I assigning it? I decided to look into the actual research around homework and found three key takeaways:

- While there is generally a correlation between homework completion and student achievement, that correlation is much greater in grades 7–12 than it is in grades K–6.
- Homework is often a source of tension between schools and homes, students and teachers, students and caregivers, and teachers and caregivers.

- The most effective homework provides students with differentiated choices.

I wasn't sure how to use this information until one day I went out for dinner and I realized that the solution to my problem was right there in front of me: a menu!

I jotted down a few ideas: Reading would be the beverage section because, just like in a restaurant, everyone needed to select from it, but they could still choose. Then they would choose from at least one of the other categories: mathematics, writing (which included inquiry), physical fitness, fine arts, and social emotional learning. My wife, a graphic designer, took my ideas and turned them into an actual restaurant-style menu.

The goal was for students to be empowered to make decisions (with adult guidance) that would help them guide their own learning. Some students chose to do math worksheets. Some chose to create projects and shared them with the class. Others invited me and their classmates to piano recitals, ballet performances, football games, and soccer matches. The homework menu was a hit with students and with caregivers!

A free downloadable template for this menu can be found in the resources for this chapter at jcasatodd.com.

ALEX T. VALENCIC, EDM, PROFESSIONAL LEARNING COORDINATOR, FREEPORT SCHOOL DISTRICT #145

DISCUSSION QUESTIONS

1. What are some of the experiences you have had around homework with parents? With students?
2. Karen maintains that being a student 24/7 is not good for her well-being. In what ways can you apply the ideas from this chapter to being a teacher 24/7? What are some boundaries you can set for the work you take home?
3. What ideas come to mind when it comes to artificial intelligence and homework?
4. What is one idea from this chapter that resonates?

CHAPTER 5

MAKE SCHOOL MORE PRACTICAL

FROM THE STUDENT'S DESK: KAREN

The day I applied for my first job the month after I graduated from high school, I realized there was a whole world I was ill-prepared for. I had no idea how to write a good résumé or cover letter. Turning to the internet to help me craft my job application was a natural step—it's something I do a lot as a first-generation student who has to figure everything out herself. Knowing how to effectively "google" my way through a problem is a life skill of mine, but there are times I wish high school taught me a little more life skills so I would feel less lost when navigating the vast world outside of being a high school student.

My high school education provided me with a strong foundation in academics. After taking so many rigorous courses in English, math, social studies, and science, I most definitely graduated at eighteen as a book-smart kid. I excelled in writing five-paragraph essays. I knew how to calculate derivatives and solve optimization problems. I could tell you about the different states of matter, Manifest Destiny, and supply and demand. But I couldn't tell you much about "being an adult."

I didn't know the difference between a due date and a statement date for credit cards. After graduating from high school, I learned that being able to use tools and software like Microsoft Excel and Adobe Creative Cloud are in-demand skills, but we didn't use these in high school. My mom, a nurse, told me one day that I should get CPR certified with her when she needs to renew her certification—I then realized that I didn't know how to respond to medical emergencies besides calling an ambulance. When I started college, I had to learn how to study effectively because college classes are nothing like high school classes. Isn't studying a skill we're supposed to master in high school?

I've heard many arguments that life skills and topics like sex education, personal finance, and diversity don't need to be taught in K–12 schools because it's the parents' responsibility to teach their children these things at home, or you'll encounter these things in college and in the real world. It's not easy to teach and assess these things in a classroom setting; however, not all families can teach their children life skills and not all students will go to college. Not all students have the privilege of having an adult figure in their life who can teach them.

I often think about the fact that we're legally adults when we're eighteen in the United States, yet we don't graduate from high school with all the knowledge and skills we need to survive adulthood. Being an adult is hard to teach in the classroom because so much of our learning about the world is through experience. But there are things that can be taught so older teens can hit the ground running: how to responsibly use credit cards, write résumés, take on student loans, buy insurance, and have healthy habits. Moreover, the skills we need today are vastly different from those students needed ten or even five years ago. For example, digital literacy is critical in a world where information is primarily diffused through digital platforms that are full of misinformation, AI-generated content, and other media we need to be able to interrogate before accepting as the truth.

The education system does a good job of developing a standard set of skills and knowledge that the general population should have about English, math, social studies, and science. However, where it fails is equipping students with a similar standard set of skills and knowledge related to their well-being and growth. I propose rethinking the current curriculum in high schools so school is more practical and teaches students the skills they need to become successful young adults in a digital and diverse world.

PRACTICAL KNOWLEDGE

My definition of "practical knowledge" is the same as what Dr. David Perkins, professor emeritus of education at Harvard University, means when he describes something as "lifeworthy." In the article "What's Worth Learning in School?" by Lory Hough, Harvard's *Ed.* magazine editor-in-chief, Perkins tells Hough that the goal in school is to have students learn as much information as possible; however, not a lot of that information is going to prepare you for life or is information you'll able to use on a regular basis, hence it lacks *lifeworthiness.*

"It's nice to know things. I like to know things. You like to know things," Perkins says. "But there are issues of balance, particularly in the digital age. The information in textbooks is not necessarily what you need or would like to have at your fingertips."[1]

I've always had a thirst for knowledge and genuinely enjoy learning new things. However, a lot of what I've learned in my many years of school has faded into obscurity after I've taken a test. I don't think about the area of curves often because I'm not studying math or engineering, and I don't think about plant cells because I'm not pursuing anything biology-related. That isn't to say topics like the Boston Tea Party and stoichiometry are irrelevant. In high school, I was always told by my teachers, parents, and peers to explore different things so I could discover what I wanted to do after I graduated. There were countless clubs I could join and advanced classes I could take to further my knowledge. I took advantage of concurrent enrollment so I could take an astronomy class at my local community college to learn more about astronomy and if I wanted to pursue a related career path. I do think it's important to learn as much as we can about the world as teens and young adults, but there's more to learning than memorizing facts.

When I asked students, "What is the purpose of school?" in my survey for this book, they had different answers that all contributed to the same bigger picture. School is where you go to become educated, be prepared for everyday life, have a better chance of getting a job, become a worker, socialize and make friends, be exposed to the basics of many subjects and fields—the responses go on and on. Their reasons are valid: we go to school to become educated on different disciplines that are meant to help us eventually find a path in life and succeed in it. If high school is meant to help students discover what their futures might look like, we should continue delivering a well-rounded and modern education and expose students to the finer details of how the world around us works. We should not only learn but also have ample opportunities to apply our knowledge to real-world situations. As a college student, for instance, my coursework is centered around projects that prepare me for my summer internships.

I want to take a moment to explain what I mean by "modern education." Perkins says in order to make school more useful, we need to ask questions about the content currently being taught and deliver more lifeworthy content. A modern education should encompass practical topics that will prepare students from Generation Z and future generations to live in a world facing unprecedented digital, environmental, social, political, and economic circumstances and problems. I won't be dissecting the curriculum in world history or chemistry in this chapter and saying what shouldn't be taught anymore because that's a conversation outside the scope of this book—this conversation involves students, teachers, parents, and education board members, among many other stakeholders. However, I do have ideas about which lifeworthy topics could be added to the curriculum.

Personal finance, for instance, would be an amazing topic to teach in school because financial literacy can change lives. According to Next Gen Personal Finance (NGPF), in 2022, eight states in the

United States required high school students to take at least one semester of a stand-alone personal finance class, and seven states began implementing personal finance curricula for high schoolers.[2] I hope to continue seeing more states across the country mandate stand-alone personal finance education for students—what I learned in AP Macroeconomics was not enough to teach me how to manage my own finances.

	2018	2019	2020	2021	2022	Future
% of U.S. high school students who graduated having taken a standalone Personal Finance course	16.4%	16.9%	18.3%	20.6%	22.7%	39.7%
States guaranteeing standalone Personal Finance courses for all high schoolers	5 STATES	5 STATES	6 STATES	7 STATES	8 STATES	15 STATES

Based on NGPF's 2022 State of Financial Education Report

Personal finance courses

Financial literacy is arguably more important for our current and upcoming generation of students than ever. Deloitte's *Global 2022 Gen Z and Millennial Survey* included 14,808 Gen Z (born between 1997 and 2012) and 8,412 millennial respondents across forty-six countries. The survey discovered that 29 percent of Gen Z and 36 percent of millennials see cost of living as their greatest concern. "Concerns about cost of living may be a symptom of the times, given high levels of inflation, but they also speak to issues that these generations have been expressing for years: they don't feel financially secure personally, and at a broader societal level, they are deeply concerned about wealth inequality," the survey reads.[3] Not to mention, as the cost of college increases, more students may turn to taking out loans and should be able to fully understand what taking on debt means.

Another impactful and practical topic to teach is emergency preparedness, which should include both medical and environmental emergencies. Basic first aid and CPR training empowers students with information and skills they can use to save lives, including their own. And on a similar note to knowing how to be prepared during a natural disaster, students would benefit from having curriculum that's centered around sustainability and environmental awareness. This may not have been a priority in the past, but our current generation of students should be well-educated on climate-related topics, especially because many young people today have some level of climate anxiety and because previous generations didn't experience this level of environmental issues.[4]

There are countless other lifeworthy topics that I think should be taught to some degree in school: goal setting, home economics, and spotting misinformation online. It would be worthwhile to ask your students what useful information they'd like to learn in school.

PRACTICAL SKILLS

When I look at what organizations and companies such as the World Economic Forum, *Forbes*, LinkedIn, and the Organisation for Economic Co-operation and Development (OECD) say are the top skills for workers in 2030, I see that what they emphasize aren't skills I've learned or practiced enough in high school. The World Economic Forum released a video in September 2022 entitled "These Are 5 Skills Kids Will Need in the Future." The five skills are creativity, digital skills, collaboration, global citizenship, and environmental stewardship.[5] In August 2022, *Forbes* published an article on the top ten most in-demand skills in the next ten years, which include digital and data literacy, emotional intelligence, flexibility, and curiosity.[6] The OECD's Future of Education and Skills 2030/2040 initiative "aims to help education systems determine the knowledge, skills, attitudes and values students need to thrive in and shape their future."[7] They identified three major types of skills for 2030: cognitive and meta-cognitive skills (e.g., learning-to-learn), social and emotional skills (e.g., empathy), and practical and physical skills (e.g., manual skills and life skills).

What struck me when I read and watched these articles and videos on the skills we need to have in the next five to ten years is that most of these skills aren't explicitly taught in schools. For example, many of these lists include digital or technological skills in some capacity. According to Adobe, the following define the three major components of digital literacy: how you consume, create, and communicate information.[8]

Almost all of my digital skills are what I've learned in school: using Google Workspace, filming and editing videos, and designing newspaper layouts. For many students, school is where they encounter and use the most technology, which is why it's the perfect place to teach students how to use the technology available to them to their advantage.

At the time I began writing this chapter, OpenAI's AI chatbot ChatGPT was released. I was disappointed by the way the education system responded by demonizing this tool with headlines such as "The End of High-School English"[9] and going as far as banning students from using it.[10] The Los Angeles Unified School District and New York City schools restricted their students' access to ChatGPT on school networks and devices in December 2022 and January 2023, respectively, on the basis that it could promote widespread cheating and plagiarism. I believe the more appropriate reaction should have been thinking about how the education system must change to adapt to new technologies such as AI. A phone created in 2025 is completely different from a phone created in 2000. The types of assignments we're given can't be the same as what they were twenty years ago (or even what they were like before widespread public access to AI). Completing homework using ChatGPT or Gemini is a valid concern for educators, but restricting students' access to the technology isn't the answer. Instead, assignments need to evolve so they can't be fully completed by AI or even so they require students to use AI, which can help students learn about the different applications of AI in the classroom and beyond.

I also noticed that some of the skills these companies and organizations identified were skills that I was discouraged from practicing in high school. Take creativity as an example: reading that this is a skill you need to be competitive in the job market gave me pause. I don't think you learn to be creative in school. As I've argued throughout this book, the education system punishes students who don't fit into the mold of an ideal student. Creativity is punished rather than rewarded because we need to stick to the rules that teachers have established, or we'll get bad grades. Problem solving is another in-demand skill, but I don't think we learn to problem solve very well in school because what we often learn is to choose the right answer out of four given choices instead of experimenting and coming up with a solution that works. I was surprised to see curiosity as a necessary skill because, in my view, grades kill students' desire to learn and engage with material and empathy. School itself can sometimes be an unempathetic, unforgiving, and inflexible environment.

As I learn more about the skills we need for tomorrow, I see a clear disconnect between what skills students gain and practice in school—a place where children, teens, and young adults spend most of their lives—and what the job market wants to see. Many of the students in my survey for this book said school is where you go to learn the skills you need to find a job. The education system needs to ensure students learn these in-demand skills, and doing so may challenge how school has been traditionally organized and conducted—for the better.

WHAT WORKS FOR ME

I advocate for changes in schools so students have sustained opportunities to learn practical topics and skills in depth, but I recognize the challenges of creating new curricula, let alone requiring students to take these classes amid their busy schedules. Subtracting from a curriculum is already hard enough because we're used to what we've been teaching and learning for the past 150 years. Adding to it is even harder.

I acknowledge the difficulty of teaching topics like health, money, digital literacy, and safety to teens because we have limited knowledge and experience, so it can be difficult to determine where to begin these conversations for this age group. It's also not something that can only be covered in one class period, and maybe not even in a week. Despite these challenges, lifeworthy topics are still worth learning in school. It is worth equipping teens with the knowledge and skills I've listed in this chapter because it helps us become independent and competent adults. I don't see any harm in learning how to read a bank statement or how to communicate well. If I'm going to be at school for forty hours a week, I'd like to learn things that will stick with me in the long term. I do see harm in our current education system that makes no room to teach students things that will help them succeed in real-world situations. There is harm in the way schools tell us we need to learn things "just because that's how it's always been" when the conditions students live in are far different from what they were decades ago (e.g., increased global connectivity and digitalization).

1. MY TEACHERS CONNECT THE MATERIAL TO REAL-WORLD PROBLEMS, CURRENT EVENTS, OR MY INTERESTS.

Victoria from Richmond Hill, Canada, responded to my survey for this book saying, "I feel as [though] school focuses on past concepts and ignores lessons that we can apply to the present time." Several students had similar feelings, expressing that they wish the information they learn in class had some sort of real-life application. I know what Victoria means. It's easy for students to question the value of the material in class when we don't have a good grasp of how we might be able to use this information once class is over. I have a hard time engaging with the material outside of class because for most of my educational career, school has been about memorization and regurgitation. In his interview with Harvard's *Ed.* magazine, David Perkins asserts that we should be making connections between class material and the world around us. He says that instead of memorizing the facts and forgetting them after an assignment, connecting the facts to an event or phenomenon happening today helps students see the relevance in the material, which will also help it stick longer.[11]

These connections are why the things I learned in my freshman AP Human Geography class have stuck with me all these years. AP Human Geography was a unique class because we learned about the modern-day results and consequences of humans that have transformed the earth throughout history. A lot of the course consisted of making these connections between the past and the present day; oftentimes, my teacher began class by playing *CNN 10*, and we'd discuss how the news coverage was related to a chapter we'd covered in class. Thanks to these connections, I still remember what I learned in that class when I read about news on the economy or environmental issues.

Not all classes are like AP Human Geography, but that doesn't mean it's impossible to incorporate more real-life examples and lessons. If teachers are trying to think of ways to make their content more engaging for students, I encourage them to consider what worries their students—what are students anxious about at school, in the community, on social media, in the world?—and use the content to help students make sense of these anxieties. It helps the material stick while teaching students a life lesson or skill. In a math class, for instance, there could be a unit that includes calculating interest, which is something many students will encounter in their adult lives when they take out student loans, use credit cards, and more. Senior English classes can spend a week going over résumé and cover letter writing to teach students this necessary skill. Encouraging students to make frequent connections between the material and real life is one of the best ways to help students see the relevance of what they're learning and even be able to use it outside of class without the need to create a new course.

2. MY SCHOOL MAKES LEARNING PRACTICAL KNOWLEDGE AND SKILLS ACCESSIBLE.

My university offers a personal finance course[12] that covers a wide range of financial topics such as banking, credit cards and credit scores, and investing. The course is online and asynchronous, and all of the lessons and activities have been recorded and developed by the university's business school. Any student can take this class for free and without officially adding it to their school schedule: all they have to do is enroll in the course on Canvas and they'll have access to all the modules, which they can complete anytime. As an incentive to get more students to take the course, students who complete it receive a free shirt.

I recognize that student interest is a major factor when deciding whether to add another section to an existing course or to create a new course altogether. There might not be a significant number of students at your school who want to take life skills courses in high school because they want more room for other classes, and that's completely understandable. It might also be impossible to incorporate a new course into students' schedules when your school already has a lot of graduation requirements. Or the process of officially adding the course is far too tedious. This is when I think my university's model for its personal finance course would work great for schools that do want to offer comprehensive instruction on personal development and life skills topics but don't have the ability to do so school-wide.

My university's personal finance course is voluntary: no one has to sign up for this course if they don't want to, but it exists for students who have an interest in learning about how to handle money. It's a zero-stakes and self-paced course, so it's a great learning opportunity because there aren't any grades or scores to stress over. It's also convenient because everything can be accessed on Canvas, the LMS we already use school-wide. Moreover, I appreciate that this course is highly accessible. I didn't have to drop any courses in my schedule to take this class, and it's zero-cost, which is a huge plus given that college classes cost money in the United States. Given that many high schools are part of a school district, it would even be possible for teachers at multiple schools and district officials to work together to create a similar online course covering life skills and make it available to all students in the district. This lessens the burden on individual schools to develop such online courses.

STUDENT SPOTLIGHT

AI plays a multifaceted role in my education, offering me opportunities to augment my learning experience. One of its most prominent functions is providing me with powerful tools for various tasks. For instance, when writing an opinion piece for why carbon tax is bad, I used AI to learn about the topic from both perspectives as a starting point before research, to be able to make my argument more powerful. AI is an intelligent digital brainstorming partner, particularly beneficial for students facing creative roadblocks or seeking fresh insights in their educational journeys. This personalized use of AI not only enhances my learning but also encourages me to explore new ideas and viewpoints.

Nonetheless, it is important to acknowledge that educators might have reservations when it comes to integrating AI into the classroom. After discussing this topic with some of my teachers, much of the skepticism arises from concerns about the accessibility AI provides, which could potentially lead to unethical practices such as cheating. To fully harness the transformative potential of AI, it becomes imperative to address these concerns and facilitate a comprehensive understanding among teachers. Demonstrating how AI can be a powerful educational tool when used responsibly is essential for building trust and fostering collaboration between teachers and AI-driven educational tools.

The significance of embracing AI in the classroom cannot be overstated, primarily because AI is undeniably an integral part of our future. Rather than imposing bans or restrictions, we need to actively leverage the capabilities AI brings to the table. AI can significantly assist students in their learning journeys, not just by providing solutions but by encouraging creativity and offering a personalized learning experience. This personalization is instrumental in addressing the varying needs and abilities of students, making it a powerful tool to bridge educational gaps and ensure that no student is left behind. In essence, the integration of AI into education is a strategic move to prepare students for the demands of the digital age and equip them with skills that are increasingly indispensable in the modern workforce. By doing so, teachers empower students to thrive in a world where AI and technology are ubiquitous, ultimately setting the stage for a more technologically literate and adaptable workforce.

GOPIKA B., TWELFTH GRADE, ONTARIO, CANADA

FROM THE TEACHER'S DESK: JENNIFER

When I read Karen's skills list, which included digital literacy and financial literacy, it reminded me of my own daughter's experience coming home from a bank and saying to me, "It's a good thing I know how to write a five-paragraph essay, but I don't know how to apply to open up a bank account!" Surely the role of school should not be so hyper-focused on such transactional skills? Shouldn't a student be able to transfer their understanding of reading informational text to a credit card statement? And yet, I wonder what role financial and digital literacy could have played in my English curriculum. After all, the curriculum required students to read a variety of texts and write for a specific purpose and audience. Could I have gotten my students to write an application for a credit card or bank account? How might teachers effectively add some of the practicality Karen and other students crave? Karen suggests it's something we can add, but I disagree with her here. We can't add anything more to our already full plates. We are already responsible for curriculum, reporting, and the well-being of our students while trying to manage special needs and behaviors as well as parent expectations. So I suggest that we assess our own practice to see what could be replaced or tweaked. If my students experience writing a literary essay and get feedback on that, what other form of writing might I give them? In what way(s) could I give my students an authentic audience for their writing? How might I help students see the connections between my subject and others? I think often, as teachers, we default to the way we have been taught without considering the world into which our students will graduate. If the skills kids will need by the time they graduate, according to the World Economic Forum, include problem solving, self-management, working with people, and technology use and development, then how can we as teachers from K–12 ensure that we are giving students the skills they need to succeed?[13] But the most fundamental question we must ask ourselves is posed by David Jakes, author of *The Design Thinking Classroom*. He says, "The fundamental question that all educators must ask is this: Is what I am doing helping students to be ready for their lives in the context of the future? Not for college, not for a job, but for a life worth living?"[14]

TRANSPARENCY AND TRANSFERENCE

We know, as teachers, that so much of what we teach *does* have value and relevance in the real world. What we are not good at is being explicit about that. We talked about metacognition (thinking about thinking) in an earlier chapter. In his book *Visible Learning for Teachers: Maximizing Impact on Learning*, John Hattie lists metacognitive strategies as fourteenth out of 150 in terms of influence on student achievement.[15] We can use reflective questions to help students make connections to the world around them.

Including a few metacognitive reflection questions at the end of a lesson not only helps students consolidate their learning, but can also help them see how what they are learning can be transferred to other courses or the world around them.

I also think that having a reflection specifically asking kids to reflect on the World Economic Forum skills will help them to understand explicitly how their assignments are helping them to develop skills that are essential to "real life."

Problem-solving	What are a few ways you had to solve problems while working on this assignment?
	How might you have solved these problems differently?
Self-management	What are the strategies you used to manage your time? What strategies did you use to stay focused?
	What is one goal you have to improve this skill next time?
Working with people	How effectively did you work with your peers? What did you do when you disagreed?
	What is one strategy you could use to become better at this skill?
Technology use	What technology tools did you use?
	Were these tools the most effective choices? What else would have worked effectively?

World Economic Forum skills questions

Another simple way to help students transfer their knowledge is by thinking about how what we are teaching can be used by students in their daily lives. For example, kids don't see the inherent value of learning about persuasive techniques in a story or article they are reading because they don't think they would ever have to do this outside of school. And yet, they will need persuasive techniques when they are trying to convince their parents to let them go to a party, persuade a friend to their point of view, or persuade someone to hire them. The same could be said about poetry; kids never felt that reading poems was relevant to their lives until I connected poetry to the songs they were listening to. One of the most successful assignments I have ever used was a poetry mash-up assignment whereby kids selected one of the poems we studied and mashed it up with a popular song. They used GarageBand on our school iPads or Soundtrap (device agnostic) to create an entirely different "poem." They saw poetry in a completely different way after that assignment and genuinely enjoyed the creation process as well.[16]

In Ontario, our revised English curriculum (grades seven through nine at the time of writing) added a specific reference to transferable skills. These are similar to twenty-first century skills or global competencies that can be seen in countless curricula around the world. The terms differ slightly, but the emphasis in this new curriculum is about ensuring kids "demonstrate an understanding of how the seven transferable skills (critical thinking and problem solving; innovation, creativity, and entrepreneurship; self-directed learning; collaboration; communication; global citizenship and sustainability; and digital literacy) are used in various language and literacy contexts."[17] As a result, I co-taught a lesson where we learned what the skills meant and then asked students in every subsequent class, via an exit card, what skills they were practicing. Doing this will go a long way toward helping kids understand why they are doing what they are doing in the classroom.

TEACH AS IF AI EXISTS–BECAUSE IT DOES

Karen mentions the open-source artificial intelligence platform ChatGPT, and by the time you are reading this, I imagine that AI will have become even more prevalent, and according to some educators, problematic. There have been countless headlines in response to ChatGPT with a fear that I can only assume happened when the printing press first came on the scene. "The College Essay Is Dead" was one of the first articles I saw.[18] I recall the first time I heard about Chat GPT : one of my twelfth grade students saying to me, "Ms. Casa-Todd, I will never again be writing an essay."

What we know at this moment in time is that AI can accomplish any traditional school task with little effort. We also know that

AI is biased, has inaccuracies (hallucinations), is difficult to detect with accuracy, and makes citation and giving credit where credit is due incredibly difficult. I also know, from personal experience, that whether or not AI is banned or whether or not teachers allow it, kids are using it. And so, if we consider that we have spent a whole chapter on feedback and other one-on-one connections, we need to think and teach differently knowing that AI exists. We need to shift our lessons so that what matters—the human teacher in the room and the human peers—are at the center of what we do in class. We need to have courageous conversations with students about how using the tool will help them to learn or prevent them from learning. Given the fact that AI can do in seconds what we traditionally have asked our students to do over the course of days or even weeks, we need to think about how AI can help us as educators streamline activities that take away our attention from our students. That way, we will be able to focus more on the kids in front of us.

The response by many districts has been to ban the platform so students can't access it at school, but all this does is prevent me from accessing it at school without switching to my data plan in order to model ethical and responsible use (an equity problem that ensures that our poorer students without data plans could not access the platform while our more privileged students could).

If our response is AI detectors, then we are missing the point, I think. Can you imagine how much time and energy I would have to spend trying to "catch" all of the cases of students using AI to do their work for them? What if instead we began with a prompt in ChatGPT and had students work on using their critical thinking skills to come up with a more specific prompt? We know that asking questions in a day and age where information is in abundance is a skill students need in life. The other way we can use AI platforms in our classes is to get students to begin there and make their responses better.[19] Gopika, who wrote the Student Spotlight earlier in this chapter, spoke to me about using AI to challenge her own biases, which I hadn't thought about before our conversation. When students enter the workforce, and depending on the career they select, they may want to capitalize on AI as a tool to help them generate ideas.

As an example, you can share how Ryan Reynolds used ChatGPT to create an ad for his company, Mint Mobile. Reynolds asked ChatGPT to write an ad "in his sardonic voice, include a joke, curse word, and let customers know Mint, unlike competitors, is still offering post-Boxing Day deals." So basically, what would take an ad agency weeks and a significant amount of money no longer requires either. The result was generated with such great accuracy that one *Forbes* writer referred to it as "mildly terrifying," while another referred to it as the "robot apocalypse." Having students reflect on these headlines would also serve as a great basis for conversation about the impact of AI on education and the world of work. Depending on when you are reading this, many more ideas for how to leverage AI in education are sure to be widely available.

A FOCUS ON MULTILITERACIES

We used to define literacy as the ability to read and write a text, which of course at its very core it is, but today, a text can be a website, a video, an image, or a meme, and literacy can take the form of critical literacy, visual literacy, cultural literacy, games literacy, information literacy, financial literacy, and on and on. Feels overwhelming, doesn't it? And yet, if we don't consider a broader definition of literacy, we will have a generation of students, like Karen, feel like what they are learning in school has little connection to what they will need in the "real world." One of my favorite definitions of literacy comes from the Alberta educational system:

> [Literacy is] the ability, confidence, and willingness to engage with language to acquire, construct, and communicate meaning in all aspects of daily living. Language is explained as a socially and culturally constructed system of

communication. It is critical in helping us make sense of the world.[20]

Simplified: literacy is the ability to read and write the world. Do students know how to *read* the Google search page and a website effectively? What are the characteristics of a credible website? Can they discern fact from fiction online? The following are a few ideas that can be implemented in any subject area and adapted for any age, but to teach multiliteracies, you must first be aware of them.

INFORMATION AND MEDIA LITERACY

A 2019 study by the Stanford History Education Group showed that high school students have difficulty discerning fact from fiction online. Joel Breakstone, one of the authors of the study and the director of the Stanford History Education Group, challenges educators. He says, "Educational systems move slowly, but technology doesn't. We need to act urgently to ensure our students' ability to engage in civic life." A previous study showed that middle-school students didn't fare any better. Another factor we need to pay attention to is that tweens and teens are getting the majority of their news from social media, including TikTok and Instagram, according to a 2022 study: "The number of people consuming news content on TikTok has increased from 800,000 in 2020 to 3.9 million in 2022. For the first time, Instagram is the most popular news source among younger people—used by 29 percent of teens—with TikTok and YouTube close behind."[21]

One of my first teaching placements was teaching a media studies class. We analyzed magazine articles and news headlines as well as television commercials. We used the media triangle to analyze what messages the creators were trying to send. If the majority of students are consuming content online and from social media, then it stands to reason that the examples we provide, in a variety of subject areas, need to help them interpret news in the form they are seeing it. I used to start with credible sources and show them why the source was credible.

Now, I begin with a tweet, blog post, TikTok, or any noncredible source and have students tell me why they can or can't trust the source. A variety of tools such as CRAAP and SOURCE, which have been used for decades, can be applied, but honestly, having worked with teenagers for as long as I have, I can tell you that few of them internalize these structures. Instead, I will often ask, *Who* is the author and *what* credibility do they have? *Why* have they written the piece? *What* are they persuading me to do? *When* was this written?

Essentially, students need to understand that every media text is a construction, that they contain value messages, that different audiences interpret media messages differently, that each medium has its own unique techniques and forms, and that all media have special interests. Whether you teach science, art, history, or literature, there is always a plethora of news to draw from. The following are media literacy questions you can ask of any media text if you have a little more time. Doing this often and cross-curricularly will develop a habit of mind that is essential for students to understand what they are viewing when it comes to media texts.

MEDIA IS A CONSTRUCT

- Who made this text (article, image, video, post, etc.)?
- What are the choices that were made in the construction of this text (colors, words, images, placement of images)?
- Whose voice is missing?

ALL MEDIA CONTAIN VALUE MESSAGES

- What is the text (article, post, image, video, etc.) trying to convince me to do?
- How do the choices in making this text (colors, words, images, placement of images) show what the author thinks or cares about?

DIFFERENT AUDIENCES INTERPRET MEDIA MESSAGES DIFFERENTLY

- How does the text (article, post, image, video, etc.) make me feel?
- How do the choices in making this text (colors, words, images, placement of images) affect how I interpret the message?
- Do I agree or disagree with the message? Why?

EACH MEDIUM HAS ITS OWN UNIQUE TECHNIQUES AND FORMS

- What would this look like if it were created as a _____ instead of _____? (For example, an image instead of an article.)
- What is the text made up of? (Colors, words, images, placement of images.)

MEDIA HAVE SPECIAL INTERESTS

- Who makes money from this text?
- How are the elements of the text (colors, words, images, placement of images) designed to grab my attention?

We can use simplified versions of these questions with students as young as first grade. It is essential that we spend time helping students to deconstruct and create media to truly understand how it works. Such an approach not only helps students gain valuable skills but positions them in their world and helps them to read the world around them.

VISUAL LITERACY

Visual literacy is defined by the American Library Association as "a set of abilities that enables an individual to effectively find, interpret, evaluate, use, and create images and visual media... A visually literate individual is both a critical consumer of visual media and a competent contributor to a body of shared knowledge and culture."[22]

Students encounter visual images in the news, as was previously referenced. And so, if we aren't helping students to deconstruct images, they are at a disadvantage when it comes to interpreting and evaluating news. At its simplest, bringing in photos and asking students to caption them can be an effective and quick critical thinking activity. The *New York Times* has a feature called "What's Going On in This Picture?" whereby on Mondays they post a photograph stripped of its caption and any other identifying information. Then students from around the world contribute captions and identify what they notice. On Thursdays, there is a "reveal." And while there is an actual answer, students get skilled at looking closely at images to make inferences.

The Friday Photo, an idea shared by Noa Daniel, is by far my favorite strategy for practicing visual literacy with students. She engages in this activity every Friday beginning in a teacher-directed way, and then by midyear, students are assigned a Friday and invited to lead the class in a deconstruction of a photo independently! Students must first describe what they see in the photo, ask questions about what they see, and make inferences, and only then are they asked to evaluate the purpose and message by giving it a creative title. This strategy could definitely be utilized to deconstruct the increasingly prevalent AI-generated images we see, as well.

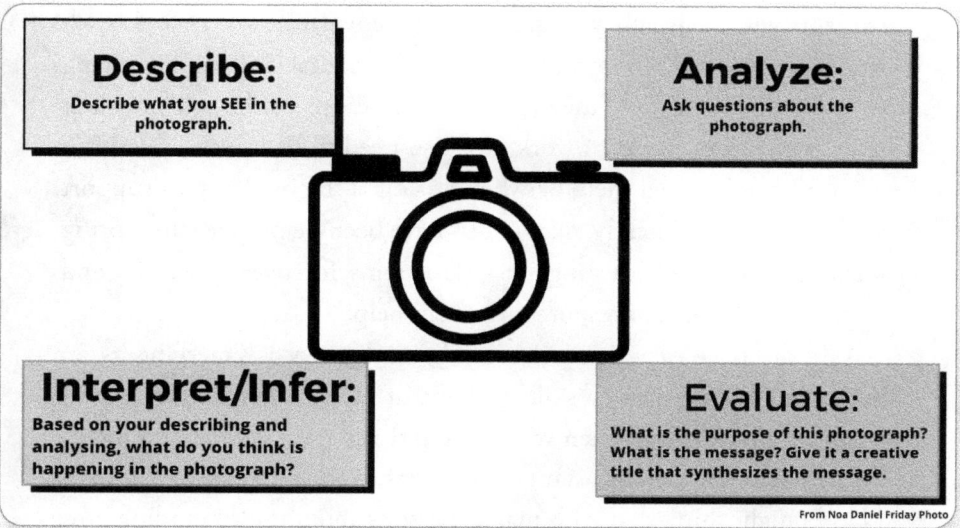

Friday Photo

Imagine if every K–12 student had the experience of Friday Photos even just once a year and how much better they would be at interpreting visual messages.

DIGITAL LITERACY

According to the American Library Association, digital literacy can be defined as "the ability to use information and communication technologies to find, understand, evaluate, create, and communicate digital information, an ability that requires both cognitive and technical skills."[23]

There is no denying that our world has become increasingly digital and students will graduate into a world where technology skills are essential. Once students have a foundation in reading and writing, we need to ask them to demonstrate their learning in a variety of formats that may include podcasts, blogs, videos, and even social media posts. Recently, I have seen a tendency in teachers to revert to paper and pencil tasks, which is not congruent with the society into which students will eventually graduate. When we use technology tools with students, we need to be explicit about the digital skill we are trying to teach them and how they can see applications of the tools in their daily lives or the world of work. We also need to be intentional about when technology will help or when analog is the best way to support student learning. Luckily, many of us have been helping teachers bring technology-enabled learning into classrooms for over a decade, and there are a plethora of resources that can help.[24]

At the time of writing this book, AI literacy is emerging as an important digital-literacy skill. In light of that, courageous conversations about knowing when to model and use AI and when to intentionally omit AI are important for teachers to consider. Many students I have taught think that AI is magic! Lessons about understanding how it works, its limitations, and its biases are also important for students who will graduate into a world in which AI is a reality.

REAL-LIFE PROJECTS SOLVING REAL-LIFE PROBLEMS

Innovate inside the Box by George Couros and Katie Novak emphasizes the extent to which our goal in education should be more about "helping students seek out problems that are meaningful to them and then finding ways to solve or respond to those issues." In their book, they share the example of Kylie Simonds, who at a very young age invented backpacks for kids undergoing chemo so they wouldn't have "cluck, ugly IV poles," as well as the example of seventeen-year-old Kenneth Shinozuka, who invented a wearable wireless sensor in response to his grandfather's nighttime wandering.

In my podcast, *Social LEADia: Celebrating Awesome On and Offline*, I was able to get to know Josh Feinsilber, founder of Gimkit. Gimkit is an educational game that is like Kahoot! but with way more opportunities for competitive fun. He told me that he found Kahoot! ineffective because you only get to answer the question once. In his iteration of the game, users encounter a question several times so they can practice and recall terms and ideas more effectively. He also added several competitive elements to it that he felt teens would enjoy more. What I found most fascinating is that the company he now runs full-time came out of a school project. You see his school, Gibson Ek, is a nontraditional one whereby students are engaged in real-life project-based learning. Their website page says, "Gibson Ek students learn through self-directed projects, incorporating reading, writing, science, social studies, and math along the way."[25] Students are also assigned mentors from regional businesses and organizations and meet with them either in person or virtually to explore career interests as well as soft skills.

I don't teach in a nontraditional school, and yet, I have encountered much success with students engaging in self-directed projects that address real-life issues or problems through the design thinking process. The real world uses design thinking as a process to identify problems and find solutions. When I had the honor of going to New York City in 2019 as part of the Google Innovator cohort, I was taken through Google's version of design thinking, which all their departments engage in when launching a product.

At my school, I use an adaptation of IDEO's format that I first created to use with students during a Digital Leadership Day to identify issues in their school around cyberbullying and other issues around school culture, which you will read about in greater detail in the next chapter.[26]

IDEA SPOTLIGHT
SPLICE PROJECTS

The SPLICE Projects initiative was conceived from a combination of inspiration and dedication. It was inspired by the work of a local private school who had removed the traditional silos created by subject periods, and it derived from a group of educators who sought to investigate the question "What would happen if students were given the opportunity to lead their own learning?" At its core, SPLICE

Projects is centered upon empowering student choice and voice, and in doing so, the result that has consistently manifested has been an increase in student commitment to learning and an increase in student engagement.

SPLICE Projects invites students to spend one week dedicated to inquiry-driven, self-directed learning, centered upon a project of their choosing. Traditional subject periods are removed, affording students the opportunity to delve deep into their projects without time constraints or interruption. School communities that have implemented SPLICE Projects have approached scheduling in different ways to best suit their individual contexts. In schools where an entire team of teachers is onboard and invested in the project, this has unfolded into full days of uninterrupted time. Other school communities, especially those working with younger students, have adopted a half-day model of uninterrupted time. And in schools where teachers were not comfortable or experienced with curriculum integration in this way, a starting point has been small SPLICE periods weekly, with less interruption to the traditional teaching and subject-period model. SPLICE Projects are not intended to be one-size-fits-all; instead, schools are encouraged to start where they are comfortable so as to begin to cultivate a culture of inquiry among their community, and hopefully, expand upon it over time.

Students are offered the flexibility to engage in projects associated with any subject or discipline, not just those commonly studied within school settings. Historically, projects have ranged across the following disciplines: building, construction, engineering, coding, robotics, 3-D design, visual arts, dramatic arts, music, dance, literary arts, culinary arts, oral communication, advertising, marketing, and campaigning. The SPLICE Projects initiative is typically rolled out across a five-week span:

- **Week 1:** Students are introduced to the idea of SPLICE Projects and invited to consider what they might wish to spend their time engaged in for their project.
- **Week 2:** Students complete a project proposal form structured around the design thinking process.
- **Week 3:** Teachers review project proposal forms and provide descriptive feedback.
- **Week 4:** This is the week of production; students engage in their self-directed learning projects, documenting their learning along the way.
- **Week 5:** Students share their projects via a reflective presentation of their learning journey.

Splice Projects transform the traditional roles of both teachers and students. Teachers are provided with an opportunity to act as mentors and to observe their students in types of learning they don't typically see within the traditional school day. Teachers can also leverage their personal talents and expertise to support students and their projects, as students are divided based on project type and grouped with a teacher who can best support their needs. Teachers are free to engage in critical dialogue and reciprocal learning with students, as they are not preoccupied by evaluative demands. The emphasis and value is placed on the learning process, rather than the final product (projects themselves are not evaluated); only the final presentation is graded. This gives students the freedom and safety to take risks and push themselves to engage in a new learning experience outside their traditional comfort zones.

MARISA BENAKIS (SHE/HER), EXPERIENCED K–12 EDUCATOR AND STREAM CONSULTANT, CO-CREATOR OF SPLICE PROJECTS AND STUDENT VOICE ADVOCATE

IDEA SPOTLIGHT
GENIUS HOUR

I am passionate about inclusion and finding ways for my littles to be able to experience everything others can. It may look a little different, but there shouldn't be age limits on experiences like this! For me, it started about ten years ago when I saw a variation of Genius Hour described on Twitter (X). It was a high school class, and I was immediately intrigued. I started gathering more info about this subject. To preface, I love learning new, innovative ways to teach my family. Yes, my family; my second graders and I are a family. :) After learning different ways educators implement this, I realized I was only seeing examples of either secondary/upper elementary or gifted learners. My thoughts were immediately "My learners can do this! All abilities can do this!"

As an intro, I read the book *The Most Magnificent Thing* to my class and we discuss the girl's mindset and her passion. Next I have chart paper around the room with questions like "What are your passions? What are your strengths? What are your stretches? What are you curious about?" The kids do a gallery walk and answer the questions with Post-it notes and then we discuss. From there the kids decide on their topic and if they will be working with a buddy or by themselves. From there we establish Fridays as our Genius Hour day, and we devote an hour each Friday to Genius Hour. Kids establish their topic and come up with a question to kick off their research. For example, a group did their Genius Hour on Arabic culture and the question was "How would you feel if you were Arabic?" This kicks off the LONG research process. :) My family uses that research to create either a Google Slides or Keynote presentation. The slides are based on the learner. There should be an activity that incorporates the learning that was just presented. For example: a group who did their project on baking brought items to make no-bake apple pie, another did theirs on football and brought supplies to showcase football skills, and so on. My kids also create their own rubric that highlights their presentation using Keynote/Google Slides: they all use the supplies and everyone is involved. Finally, we cover presentation skills: loud, clear, upbeat, and able to answer questions. There is also a QR code on their rubric that showcases their personal video, which they use as a personal reflective diary during this whole process.

In any setting, with any ability, Genius Hour is a great way to engage, motivate, and empower our kids to use their voice and teach their family on a subject they are passionate about!

Differentiation is baked into every concept of Genius Hour! In Genius Hour, kids also learn about social skills, leadership, cooperation skills, and navigating the web. Learners will gain the confidence, spark of learning, and love of school again![27]

MELISA HAYES (SHE/HER), EXPERIENCED SECOND GRADE EDUCATOR AND AUTHOR, @MRSHAYESFAM

DISCUSSION QUESTIONS

1. What resonated with you when you read Karen's experiences?
2. What are a few ways you can be transparent and explicit about how skills in your subject connect to students' daily lives?
3. How can you have courageous conversations about the impact of AI on learning and assessment?
4. What is one idea showcased in this chapter that you can use or modify for your context?

CHAPTER 6

STUDENT VOICE, CHOICE, AND AGENCY

FROM THE STUDENT'S DESK: KAREN

I began this book with a memorable learning experience: a research project I did on dinosaurs in elementary school. In middle school, I did a group project where we designed a trip to Mars, and I worked with a friend to create a hydroponic garden for the eighth-grade science fair (it was quite labor-intensive and expensive for thirteen-year-olds, but we won a medal for our hard work!). The group video project I did in my first high school Spanish class is my favorite video project to date (video projects are my least favorite group assignments, so that's saying something). The monthslong research paper I wrote on the novel *Earthlings* at the end of my freshman year of college is one of my best pieces of writing yet. I really hate reading my old writing, but I can tolerate that paper.

Something all these assignments have in common is that they gave me a lot of choices. I had free rein over how I wanted to meet a set of requirements provided by my teacher. Sometimes it was hard to get started. In elementary school, I usually struggled because I had all these ideas I wanted to pursue and needed to pinpoint which one was the most viable. In high school, this became a struggle that stemmed from not being used to being creative anymore (and from fixating on the grade I wanted). I didn't know where to begin when I had such open-ended assignments because school trained me to follow instructions to a T. I always expected assignments to be predictable and come with a clear set of directions because that's what the majority of my high school work was like. Open-ended assignments that gave me a choice always gave me a lot of anxiety and stress. I saw them as a hassle to complete because they demanded more from me than most of my other assignments. I didn't like making choices. I was fifteen, sixteen, seventeen, and eighteen years old, and I wasn't used to making choices. It's a bit ironic considering decision-making is a big part of critical thinking and creativity (skills we're meant to learn in school), yet I grew to favor situations and assignments where the road to an A was clear-cut.

Much of my K–12 education was saturated with situations where I did not have a choice in how I wanted to learn something, but I do remember one assignment where I did have a choice and chose to turn in something disappointing. At the end of my freshman-year English class, my teacher let us create anything we wanted to represent what we learned after reading *The Immortal Life of Henrietta Lacks*. My partner and I wanted to do something easy. We wrote an article, designed a one-page newspaper, and turned in that piece of paper while our peers went all out and created beautiful arts and crafts. Put simply, our project was lame.

I should've taken advantage of this opportunity to tap into my personal creativity, but I struggled because, in my experience, so much of the traditional education system permits little choice, making me feel like my opinions and interests aren't valued. If I'd had more choice in how I wanted to learn, I might've engaged enthusiastically and produced something important to me and showcased my learning. Instead, I created something that meant nothing to me.

THE MOST IMPORTANT STAKEHOLDERS WITH THE SMALLEST VOICES

At the middle school and high school I went to, students could take on a more active role on campus and participate in improving students' experience by joining the student government. However, student government activities (assemblies, spirit weeks, senior events, etc.) don't impact what happens inside the classroom. Dana Mitra, a professor of education at Pennsylvania State University and longtime advocate for student voice in school, makes a point that student government (a traditional leadership role for students) is "categorically different" from student voice initiatives that seek to address and improve school and classroom problems in her article "Amplifying Student Voice." Mitra writes that "at the simplest level, student voice initiatives give young people the opportunity to share with administrators and faculty their opinions about school problems. In more extensive student voice initiatives, students collaborate with adults to address significant problems in their schools. And in rare cases, students assume leadership roles in change efforts."[1]

In the introduction of this book, I argued that students are the most important stakeholders in the education system because we're the ones who are most directly impacted by it. I first want to focus on the lack of student choice on a smaller scale, the classroom, and how it negatively affected my learning.

Students are the ones who sit in the classroom every day and receive the education that's been shaped by other stakeholders: teachers, parents, school board members, and state and national departments of education, to name a few. I don't like the schooling environment, but I'm always surprised and impressed that there's so much information in the world for us to learn. I know it must be hard to develop a curriculum because you can't teach us everything. I should be excited about this because I love to learn and want to know about everything there is to know, but I'm not. Most of the time in high school, I felt unstimulated.

It sounds weird coming from me because I took so many honors and Advanced Placement classes that are meant to be challenging. Don't get me wrong, they were hard, but I only felt engaged during the occasional open-ended, group, or project-based assignments because almost everything else we did bored me: the readings, worksheets, tests. I noticed that most of the assignments that made me feel this way were the ones that didn't give me the opportunity to create something with what I learned. These were the assignments you do in a day or so, turn in, and forget about for the rest of your life, like answering questions from the textbook or filling out a study guide for the upcoming test. I knew I wasn't going to make anything meaningful out of these assignments, so I made the decision to not engage much with the material. I didn't have the time, energy, or desire to do "too much." I did just enough to get an A and move on with my life.

My attitude was far different when I had an assignment that demanded more from me. These were the assignments I listed at the beginning of this chapter, and from what I remember, they were all project- or research-based. I normally had a terrible reaction to them when I first started because as much as our typical assignments bored me, I preferred them because they were easier to complete and it was easier to predict my grade. My attitude gradually changed when I got sucked into these project- and research-based assignments because they reminded me of what it's like to learn about something that interests you and to create something with your peers. When my Spanish 1 teacher assigned us a group video project, I instantly felt dread and wished we could just do more pages in our practice book as we'd always done. I ended up having so much fun when I made this video with my groupmates. I was also extremely engaged with the material. We bounced ideas back and forth, wrote the script together, directed the filming, and even improvised on the spot. I was more confident in my Spanish and proud of what we had achieved together. As Sophia Wu, a computer science student at the University of London, told Harvard Business Publishing in the 2022 article "Why Your Students

Are Disengaged," "I would feel more engaged if professors relied less on lectures and leaned into more opportunities that allow students to actually apply the learning to projects or case studies. When I'm able to see the results of what I'm learning, I find that I'm a lot more excited to experiment and learn about the material even beyond the classroom setting."[2]

Sophia's words resonate with me, and I especially emphasize the need for more project-based assignments in school so they don't feel so uncomfortable and foreign. Like Sophia, I've felt disengaged in my college courses, particularly in my lower-division courses, because of the lack of opportunity to practice the material in practical settings. However, in my upper-division courses, the bulk of the work I do is project work, oftentimes in teams. My instructors strive to emulate what it's like to work in an industry where you get put on a team and collaborate with your colleagues to achieve something. Over time, I've become much more comfortable with open-ended assignments and value the creativity they permit. Group project work does get stressful, but I always leave learning so much from my professors and peers and feel well-prepared for future courses and my career.

In high school, open-ended assignments typically seized me with anxiety and frustration because I was so used to being told what to do. It took a while for me to retrain myself to get used to making decisions and creating something. By the time I finished these assignments, it was back to memorizing for exams and doing worksheets, whereas in college I can now expect to continue applying the material I learn to projects that are relevant to me.

I believe part of having more student voice in the classroom makes learning more student-centered because learner-driven education revolves around students pursuing what they're passionate about. This book is the product of an assignment called the Question Exploration that I did in my AP English Language class, which will be explained in Sean Ziebarth's Idea Spotlight later in this chapter. If I'd had more agency and autonomy in my learning from the beginning, I think I would've embraced and preferred open-ended assignments or at least wouldn't have been so scared of them. However, that was never the case because school was always so predetermined and teacher-centered for me. A lot of the work I did in my classes had an outcome we could predict, and we were rarely given the opportunity to make choices about how we wanted to learn something.

To be clear, this isn't to villainize the traditional mode of teacher-centered instruction and to completely do away with all assignments that aren't project-based. Tom Sherrington's 2019 essay "Myth: Teacher-Led Instruction and Student-Centred Learning Are Opposites" explains school is a combination of both. "In reality, in a school curriculum that is rich and broad, leading to deep learning, both teacher-led learning and student-centeredness will be woven together; blended and sequenced; integrated in a proportionate manner," Sherrington writes.[3] He also says, "Successful learning is always inherently student-centred. Teachers cannot be said to have undertaken successful instruction unless their students, as individuals, have secured successful learning—and this requires their active involvement, their mental engagement, their conscious effort, and active schema-building."[4] I concur with his views because the various student-centered assignments I've had were teacher-led to some extent, and having those expectations from my teachers helped give me a sense of direction. As a student, I don't know everything, and it is hard to learn something new outside of the classroom. I've taken a few online courses, and they make me appreciate the structure of sitting at my desk with my peers and teachers.

I've focused on my lack of voice in the classroom (not having a say in how I want to learn), but students also have a limited voice when it comes to problems or changes on a school-wide level. In the article "A Student's View: Young People Are the Biggest Stakeholders in Any School. They Deserve a Seat at the Decision-Making Table" by Joshua Dantzler, we learn how student voice can change the way schools work. Dantzler wrote this article when he was a university student and a member of the nonprofit Student Voice.

He shares his experiences as an actively involved student, how he listened to students' frustrations about dress codes, the lack of racial representation among staff, and what it was like to be the only minority student voice in the room: "It is fundamentally unacceptable to have a meeting about students with only one student voice in the room. Especially in something as important as education, there's always a need for new, diverse perspectives. As a result of the socioeconomic, racial, and geographic diversity of our country, our educational system encompasses people with countless different experiences. The only way to amplify the voices of all students is to include those experiences and perspectives in the conversation."[5]

I couldn't agree with Dantzler more. Throughout this book, I've identified a small number of problems students experience regularly in school. There are many more issues, some of which are unique to a school or a group of students and some of which I've never experienced. In order for these issues to be resolved—to improve school and even reform the education system—students need to be able to share their opinions and be involved in how schools plan to address these problems. Students need to be involved in meaningful and sustained ways—it's not enough to send an online survey out to students and call it a day. My high school held House of Representatives[6] meetings four times a year with students. Each third-period class nominated one student to attend these meetings. This student was responsible for gathering questions or concerns from classmates and presenting them at the House of Representatives meeting, where teachers and school administrators were also present. It functioned a lot like a town hall, and I think a space like this is a good place to start to increase student voice and invite students to co-collaborate to create solutions for problems they see on campus.

WHAT WORKS FOR ME

There are schools that are based on a student-centered or democratic model in which students not only have autonomy over how and what they learn but also how school is run: Sudbury Valley School in Massachusetts, High Tech High in California, A. S. Neill Summerhill School in Suffolk, England, to name a few. The truth is these types of schools are harder to come across or are inaccessible (e.g., cost money, have long waitlists). Most schools, especially public schools, are "conventional" in that they have an inherently adult-centered culture and don't allow students to play a bigger role in creating their education.

I would love to see more and more schools and education as a whole prioritize student voice and take major steps to facilitate learning environments where both teachers and students work together. I don't doubt that there are many school administrators and educators who want to involve students more but face barriers such as limited resources, large class sizes, bureaucracy, and perhaps lack of student interest altogether. Transforming your school to adopt Sudbury Valley School's or High Tech High's model might not be possible, but as we've said throughout this book, there are small changes that can push classrooms and schools as a whole to value and respect student voice more and increase student representation.

1. MY TEACHERS ENCOURAGE SELF-ASSESSMENT OR SELF-REFLECTION.

I mentioned earlier in this book that when my high school teachers asked me questions like "How did you grow in this course?" at the end of the semester, I made up random answers because I didn't engage enough to grow.

In college, I take these questions and evaluations more seriously, particularly when I have group projects. Half of my undergraduate education is completing group projects that are open-ended and student-driven. It's up to us to be adults and collaborate to make a project that works. Sometimes it can get messy as we iterate over and over until we reach the end goal, but that's part of learning. Simple check-ins with my teaching staff and team evaluations also helped me take more ownership of my learning. Doing these reflections reminds me that instead of being guided by instructional staff and following a plan they made for us, I worked with my peers to create our own instructional plan. Now I had to think about what worked and what didn't so I knew what to do differently when the next project came around.

My point is instead of asking students once at the end of the semester to self-reflect and then submit a vague and thoughtless answer, integrate self-reflection into the semester more often when it's relevant (i.e., when students are in charge). Again, I believe projects are a great opportunity for this. Doing check-ins with students not only adds more guidance into the process for those who may need more support, but it also encourages students to take more ownership of their learning by deciding what they're going to do next. By reflecting on the learning process, what went well and what didn't, students can make choices about what they're going to do differently to meet their goals on a future assignment that will allow them to apply the knowledge and skills they've acquired.

On a similar note, I also urge educators to ask students for feedback on assignments or the class as a whole. One thing you can do is make a feedback form for assignments through Google Forms and keep it open the entire semester. Students should have the option to submit feedback on an assignment anonymously. At the end of the semester, a more structured feedback form that asks questions about specific aspects of the class and how it can be improved next semester or next year can be released, too. This involves students in the planning and design of the curriculum and classroom.

2. MY TEACHERS LET ME CHOOSE HOW I WANT TO LEARN SOMETHING.

It makes me a bit sad to say that not many teachers have given me this type of choice. A good 80 percent of my high school assignments gave me no choices whatsoever. I wouldn't say that every assignment needs to give students options, but when it comes to large or cumulative assignments, it would be a great idea to let students decide how they want to showcase their mastery of the learning objective.

Student choice was the basis of my high school and college assignments that asked students to create anything they want to demonstrate what they've learned from the unit or course as a whole. I've come to appreciate how these assignments give us the ability to choose how we want to represent our thoughts and knowledge about the course material. It helps me feel more ownership over my learning. If educators want to provide students with a bit more structure, they can have their students submit their ideas for feedback and the green light.

Student choice can be incorporated in the classroom even outside of projects. For example, a lot of the work students do in school is group work or discussions with their tablemates. In my AP English Language class, taught by Sean Ziebarth, my peers and I generated questions that we could explore together when we were about to read a new book. Mr. Ziebarth explains the Question Formulation Technique in more detail later in this chapter. I loved doing this because we got to decide what we wanted to focus on as we read the book. It was different from what I was used to: my teachers deciding beforehand what we needed to know without listening to us. I know making teaching plans is laborious and your plans don't always go as expected, but I believe there is room to consult students and let them make decisions about their education, such as brainstorming learning goals at the beginning of a unit.

FROM THE TEACHER'S DESK: JENNIFER

When organizing this book, I wondered if student voice and agency needed to be the first chapter because it permeates everything that Karen has shared about her experiences of school. I have wondered to myself: If Karen had more say in her education, if her voice was truly valued, would she have felt compelled to write this book at all? I can tell you that my motivation for cowriting this book is because, like Karen, I don't believe we involve students enough in school.

Karen references the work of Dr. Dana Mitra, professor and founding editor of the *International Journal of Student Voice*, whose work has impacted my own thinking around student voice and agency for several years. In her article "Student Voice in Secondary Schools," she shares a hierarchy of student voice:[7]

At the bottom of the figure is listening. Listening is about students sharing their voices and opinions, while adults interpret information and possibly act on it.

Next is collaboration, which is defined as adults and youth working together, whereby adults initiate the relationship and ultimately have the final say in what happens.

Mitra places leadership at the top of the student voice pyramid. In leadership, students make decisions while the adults assist. She clarifies that most examples exist outside of school, but that there is greater benefit to youth and adults alike if this model is assumed in school transformation.

Practically, this is what the hierarchy looks like. When I interviewed forty-eight eleventh- and twelfth-grade students during their spare period to inquire about what makes the biggest difference in their learning, I recorded their responses and thematically summarized the results, which I shared on my blog and with my colleagues. I was *listening*. Did anything change? Not really, even though I shared my insights with the principal at the time. School climate surveys feel the same to me (and obviously to Karen as well). The input may change something in the future, but it does not have any immediate impact on teaching and learning. We also have monthly meetings with our homeroom reps (similar to the House of Representatives idea Karen mentions). I love that we have a greater number of student representatives give us input, and it's been a great way to foster leadership and build connections with students, but it still falls under listening according to Mitra's hierarchy.

When I invited a student to co-teach a lesson in an art class, we were collaborating.[8] The teacher I was working with was open to having a student join us as we co-planned a lesson on how to create a blog for their visual arts creations. The student gave us her expertise and showed us how to use Tumblr (which was popular at the time), and although we learned so much from her, we as teachers gave it the golden seal of approval and created a teacher example. Sometimes, we invite students to give input on school decisions or be a part of committees. This feels like collaborating as well; students see that they are a part of the process, but that the adult is the ultimate authority.

Leadership, for the most part, does sit outside of school. In working with the student council at my school, I was able to see students plan and implement initiatives, but as Karen alludes to, this impacts only a small part of the school population and is a co-curricular activity. One excellent example of student leadership happened with our antibullying committee. Rather than bring in an outside organization to teach workshops, one student asked, "Can't we create workshops and teach them?" Why not? Our principal, who is an advocate for student voice, not only loved the idea but helped facilitate the planning with the students. Our students drafted lessons, got feedback from us (the teachers), practiced their workshops, and got feedback from their peers and then facilitated workshops in tenth-grade classes. The euphoria when we debriefed was palpable. One student in particular, Amanda, in her final reflection said she had never considered herself to be a leader and expressed how proud she was not only of the lesson her group created but her ability to connect with the younger students. It is an experience which can easily be replicated.

Before you read the additional ideas I share, think about the hierarchy of student voice and what this looks like in your classroom, in your school, and in your district, and where there might be room for student voice in the form of leadership. I was a part of an AI steering committee within my district. The committee consisted of senior administration, IT, union representatives, a few district consultants, and both secondary and elementary teachers. I think they maybe regretted inviting me to be a part of it, because I asked why students weren't at the table and pushed to find out at what stage in creating a policy for AI for our district students would be involved since not only are they direct stakeholders, but the ways in which they use AI (age restrictions notwithstanding), present an important lens. At every level, you will encounter educators who believe we have actually come too far in education and that students have too much power, or who don't recognize the value of including them. This is a pity, because in my experience, when you do invite students to the table, they add so much value and perspective.

SELF-DIRECTED LEARNING

Karen talks about the most memorable projects she experienced in school as ones that allowed her to choose her own topic and engage in research that was self-directed with iteration that allowed her to self-assess and embrace mistakes. Although choice boards in previous chapters allow for student choice and voice, what students are required to complete is generally dictated by the teacher. This is, of course, fine for many assignments. It would seem, however, that all of those memorable projects in Karen's school career took the form of project-based learning, inquiry learning, or design thinking structures that have a level of autonomy and personalization that choice boards do not necessarily offer.

Project-based learning is defined by PBLWorks as "a teaching method in which students gain knowledge and skills by working for an extended period of time to investigate and respond to an authentic, engaging, and complex question, problem, or challenge."[9] Inquiry-based learning, according to Queen's University Centre for Teaching and Learning, is "based on John Dewey's philosophy that education begins with the curiosity of the learner, [and] places the responsibility for learning on the students and encourages them to arrive at an understanding of concepts by themselves." In inquiry-based learning, "students are supported in developing their abilities to: ask good questions, determine what needs to be learned and what resources are required in order to answer those questions, and share their learning with others."[10] Design thinking "can be defined as a mindset and approach to learning, collaboration, and problem solving. In practice, the design process is a structured framework for identifying challenges, gathering information, generating potential solutions, refining ideas, and testing solutions."

Both the Idea Spotlights in the previous chapter (Genius Hour and Splice Week) also center on formats that allow for students to engage in a topic that interests them that is connected to their own world, but they also allow students to self-direct their learning. What all of these structures have in common is that they are driven by a problem or challenge students perceive, and they culminate in a project or innovation that addresses that problem. In the process of coming to a solution, students have to research extensively, iterate, test, get feedback, and try again. Ideally, kids also get to see their innovation take action in the world.

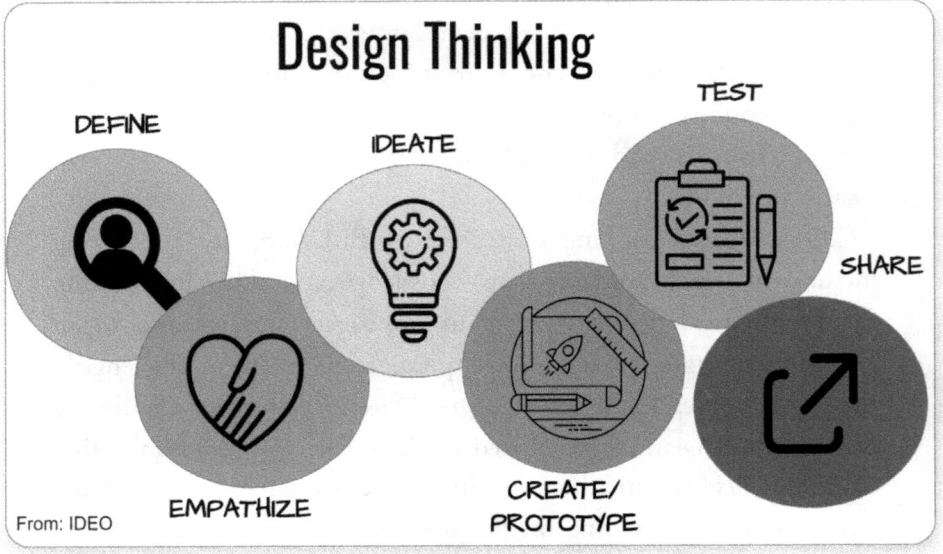

Design thinking by IDEO

I have used design thinking projects over other structures because students define their own problems connected to curriculum expectations and thus design thinking allows for the integration in a variety of subject areas. As I mentioned in the last chapter, my first experience implementing this approach was with a group of students in Wisconsin. Students from several middle schools and two high schools spent the day learning about students who were using technology and social media for good and leading in online spaces. They listened to a keynote by me about digital leadership and learned about cyber safety. They then took their learning and ideas and put them in action by first coming up with a problem unique to their school and deciding who would be helped by their idea (empathy). They then went back to test, iterate, and implement their ideas. There was a teacher from each school who could guide students, but ultimately students took ownership of the problems and the solutions. In fact, the best projects have been ones where kids think about the problems in their own school or community in order to create solutions. Most recently, I had the honor of leading students in Nebraska in a similar process, and I can't wait to see their projects take form.

I have also used design thinking in particular in science classes as students come up with ideas for addressing climate change in our community and in our school, and in religion classes in the context of addressing the global goals. It is one of the only structures that truly allows students to make mistakes, test out designs, and create something of value. One group who focused on the excessive use of plastic bags repurposed the bags into interesting jewelry, which they then sold. Another group focused on the negative impact of fast fashion and repurposed T-shirts into tote bags and pencil cases. One group created a campaign to collect and donate shoes for the homeless after empathizing with a homeless person who might be lacking comfortable shoes.

Technology tools which allow students to collaborate online but not necessarily in real time have allowed my students to get input from other classes around the world. I leveraged my own network on social media to have high school students from Malaysia and Vancouver, Canada, provide feedback on student prototypes. When I found out that Melisa Hayes's class (you met her in our Spotlight in the last chapter) was also creating prototypes for climate change, we collaborated briefly with them as well. Although the timing wasn't quite right for this year's projects, I love the idea of having older students work with younger students, and in today's landscape where global collaboration is a click away, making this happen will be a priority for us next year. Student reflections at the end of the unit showed the extent to which they enjoyed the freedom of topic and the global collaboration.

> **What I really enjoyed about this unit (and why)**
>
> 19 responses
>
> I loved the format of the CPT. Having each part due at a date really kept me focused and made sure that I was on task.
>
> I enjoyed that the unit was done independently since it is not a unit that requires formulas and diagrams
>
> I enjoyed the idea of getting creative and coming up with our own ideas.
>
> I really enjoyed how we got to interact with students outside of our area and got to research how we can create something that improves climate change.
>
> I liked that we had the freedom to come up with our own invention
>
> I liked listening to students from different countries and getting their perspectives to the projects/ideas that we had. I also liked how we got to be creative and push ourselves to think and improve the quality of the Earth either for us, the Earth or the animals.
>
> I really enjoyed having the freedom to come up with an invention/innovation on our own and being able to choose what goal we wanted to focus on. I also really liked how we were able to receive feedback from so many people, including from Malaysia and Vancouver.

Student reflections

There is opportunity for cross-curricular collaboration in these structures as well. Last semester, we combined a science class and a marketing class that were scheduled during the same period so the students in the science class could focus on creating a prototype and the students in the marketing class could generate marketing materials to help spread awareness in the school community. The teachers and I constantly talked about the way the students were engaging with curriculum, subject-specific vocabulary, and core concepts in a way that can't happen in traditional models. The student feedback for that project was positive as well. Our marketing students had a real "client" as a result of the success of this project. One of the coolest experiences for myself and my students was an entrepreneurial project whereby students used the design thinking framework to create a solution to a real problem in our community. Students were able to present a business plan, get a budget, assess risk, and actually create the product (in our case an app for students to help with school communication). Part of the process involved meeting with a privacy officer, a coder, and the school principal to get more information about how to build their prototype. The students involved in this project graduated this past year and in their goodbye to me shared how powerful that experience was and how much it stood out against everything else they had accomplished in high school.

Students used all five of the World Economic Forum skills we talked about in the previous chapter and more!

SHIFTING THE POWER

Cornelius Minor, author of *We Got This*, offers much insight into how we can shift the power dynamic in the classroom. As part of Matt Miller's Ditch Summit, Minor says, "It's not about giving students choices, it's about allowing them to step into their power." Wow.

In his book, Minor gives the example of having a class meeting for kids to help him with a dilemma he is having with his sister or a friend. As kids give him advice, he listens intently for what is important to his students, for how they resolve conflict, and for what they value. He is then able to draw on that information later. He has class meetings on the way to the gymnasium or as the class is transitioning. He says, "These class meetings exist for the explicit purpose of maintaining community. Kids want to be powerful, and these meetings function as a site where that power can live and grow in a democratic way."[11]

Minor also speaks a great deal about the importance of listening: informal listening in particular. He suggests that informal listening will allow teachers to "make active and long-standing adjustments to the classroom community, to our actual teaching, and to how the department, grade, or school operates."[12] Together, class meetings and informal listening will help kids gain confidence in using their voices.

Another way to shift the power in the classroom is to allow students to make decisions about what they want to learn. A 2020 qualitative study by America's Promise Alliance found that "building adults' capacity to share power with young people in ways that go beyond 'listening' enable[s] young people's agency, nurture[s] their identity development, and co-create[s] meaningful learning experiences that serve their present and future selves."[13] This supports the findings by Mitra and the hierarchy of student voice.

Our curriculum tells us what to teach, but the way in which we go about it is completely up to us. We already learned about the important role of social emotional learning in a previous chapter. In this chapter, we will talk about how students can hold a primary role in curriculum planning and implementation. When I was the literacy consultant for our district, I had the privilege of working with a teacher to test out an approach to teaching ninth-grade applied English that put students at the center of planning. This is an overview of what we did:

> **Introductory note to teachers:**
> Rather than organize the ENG1P course into the traditional units (Short Stories, Non-fiction, Plays, etc.) as has been the norm for the past twenty years, the idea for this approach is to organize the course into different guiding questions using multi-genre and multi-modal content to explore big ideas or essential questions. This approach may address frequent absenteeism, and it supports the student-centered approach that is the hallmark of modern learning.
> - Sample big ideas: Where is technology taking us? How do we embrace differences? Is music a universal language? Is family loyalty more important than friendship?
>
> **Backward Design:**
> - What do we need to know, understand, and be able to do by the end of this course? (Curriculum Expectations)
> - How will we get there? (Content, Essential Questions)

- How will we get there successfully? (Mindsets and Metacognition)

On day 1, we gave groups a copy of the Curriculum Expectations cut into strips and asked them to sort them in a way that made sense to them (they could do this electronically). We explicitly talked about how to reach consensus in a respectful way. We then asked them to record examples of the kinds of activities they had done in the past that allowed them to meet the expectations they sorted.

On day 2, we began the class with the Big Ideas/Essential Questions that might frame the course. We provided six and left one blank so students could write their own essential question. From there, each student was given five dots that they could use to "vote" for their favorite. We also invited students to add song, story, or movie ideas to each page. From this activity, we co-constructed the course outline, beginning with the big idea with the most votes.

On day 3, students learned about growth and fixed mindsets and the impact these mindsets have on learning.

Initially, if I'm being honest, it was way more work because we couldn't plan the course until we met our students, but for the rest of that year, we marveled at the extent to which students were invested in the course because they felt like they were the ones who actually created it.

Shifting the power is a tough idea for some teachers and leaders (at least that has been my experience). Any committee at our school that is teacher-run, in my opinion, should have students at the table. Every. Single. One. Without their voices at the table, we are doing exactly what Karen is suggesting at the beginning of this chapter: we are excluding a very important stakeholder. I have been fortunate in my career to have worked with many student leaders, and I know that their contributions are valuable. But you know what? Our students who don't necessarily see themselves as leaders or ones who are disengaged are the BEST kids to ask. Often, an informal wondering is more effective than a formal meeting or survey. Kids just think differently than we do; sometimes they don't have the big picture or level of maturity to get us to Mitra's leadership tier, but even listening is better than not. Our go-to question at every level of education should be "How might we get student perspectives and feedback on this?"

GIVE STUDENTS OWNERSHIP OF PHYSICAL SPACES

When I was given the go-ahead to renovate our Library Learning Commons, I collaborated with an interior design class to redesign the space.[14] In groups, they were tasked with interviewing students to find out what they wanted changed and what they wanted us to keep, and they took measurements of the physical space, designed and priced furniture, created a 3-D sketch of what they imagined the library should look like, and then pitched their designs to me, the principal, and their interior design teacher. We took elements of each of the designs and used the student furniture proposals. The impact of this process has been tremendous. In addition to our big renovation, we connect with the manufacturing class as well as the Visual Arts Council every year to add art or additional elements to our space. Our giant chessboard and Lego table were both created by students, any artwork in the library is student created, and any books or games we purchase are suggested by students.

It always amazes me to see teachers coming in early to "decorate their classroom" in preparation for students without knowing and missing valuable information about their learning needs: Will my students need fewer anchor charts on walls because they get easily distracted? Would they appreciate having their favorite quotes on the walls instead of ones I value? How would they like to see the furniture organized so they are the most comfortable? Having students make decisions in terms of what their space looks like will allow them to feel like it truly is their space.

IDEA SPOTLIGHT
CLASSROOM COMMITTEES

When I was a classroom teacher, my sixth-grade students were always eager to help me with displaying their work, tidying up, or distributing and collecting items. With this in mind, I reflected on how this particular group of students would be able to contribute to the classroom community in ways that were more impactful. I didn't mind that these students wanted to help with the aforementioned items, but I knew that I could harness this spirit of volunteerism to have them do something personally meaningful that aligned with their strengths and interests. This is where the idea of classroom committees emerged. Together as a class, we discussed classroom operations and responsibilities, which included things like managing our classroom blog, preparing our prayer table, organizing technology and providing assistance to peers, motivating each other in daily physical activity, and creating and maintaining a welcoming classroom space through bulletin board design and motivational posters. After deeper reflection, it dawned upon me that prior to introducing classroom committees, these were all *my* responsibilities as a teacher, and I gave little consideration to student voice in the planning of these items.

While I relinquished my control and management of these responsibilities, students felt empowered to take on these tasks. It was their voice that was now authoring the blog and related tweets (which I still monitored), it was their vision that directed the layout and organization of the classroom walls, it was their knowledge (from classroom lessons and their own experience) that was applied to set up our prayer table and ensure our classroom was eco-conscious, and it was their ideas that determined how we would start each morning in daily physical activity. Through this process, students worked collaboratively in small groups to determine how these responsibilities would be divided, they developed meaningful

HOPES FOR SCHOOL

relationships with their peers because they were each working toward a common goal, and they developed a sense of pride in knowing that this classroom was truly their own—from the work and quotes that adorned the walls to the knowledge that was shared via daily physical activities, the prayer table, and the blog. Students were so enthusiastic about their responsibilities in these committees that they began to see for themselves how committees could work together to improve each other's work. For example, the Information and Technology Department supported the Public Relations Department in updating the classroom blog, while the Public Relations Department checked in with the Health and Wellness Team to see if they wanted to communicate information on the blog.

Through these intersections, students developed a strong sense of community and an awareness that working together was necessary in order to advance the shared goals of the classroom.

ROBERT CANNONE (HE/HIM), OCT,
ELEMENTARY PROGRAM CONSULTANT
K-8: CURRICULUM & ASSESSMENT

IDEA SPOTLIGHT
QUESTION FORMULATION TECHNIQUE

The easiest way to make space for student voices is to simply ask for them. Midway through every school year, I ask my students to complete an anonymous evaluation of my classroom practices. I base my questions on Tripod's framework for effective teaching (bit.ly/tripod-questions). I review the results with my students, and I print out their most helpful suggestions and keep them in the front of my planner, referring to them daily.

But it was Yong Zhao who deepened my understanding of student voice when he wrote how it "requires a deep reconsideration of the role of students in the school, not as a place that transmits knowledge, but as a community of learners." I realized I was doing a disservice to my students if I only taught them what I noticed in a novel, what I was struck by in a story, or what experts who came before me had discovered. Around this same time I was introduced to Dan Rothstein and Luz Santana's *Make Just One Change*, which details a process called the Question Formulation Technique. I took it to my students immediately, and before each novel we read, students brainstormed questions they had about a topic raised by the book. Now each student had their own personalized reason to read the novel.[15]

Generating Questions

Ask as many questions as you can based on the question focus.

Do not stop to answer, judge or discuss the questions.

Write down every question exactly as it is stated.

QFT question formulation technique (shared by @MrZiebarth)

It transformed my classroom. Our class discussions no longer revolved around the details and flourishes I thought were important, details on which I had previously tested their power of memorization through multiple-choice exams. They revolved around ideas students had discovered as they explored their questions. They revolved around connections students made as they read poems, essays, and articles, listened to music and podcasts, viewed artwork and movies they found as they continued to explore their own questions. We gathered those sources into our own virtual textbook and I began learning from my students as they learned from me. We truly became a community of learners.

Student work

At the end of this process, students reported back on their journeys in myriad ways, ways they chose: sculpture, painting, podcasts, blog posts, presentations, games, videos. The quality of work they submitted followed the typical spectrum, but I was surprised and dazzled by far more assignments than ever before. And others noticed. Some of my students won writing contests for their work, others presented theirs at professional conferences, and some

explored their questions far beyond my classroom—this book you're reading is an example of how one student's question blossomed and grew. Giving students true choice and agency over their learning helps them create knowledge, developed from, as artist Claes Oldenburg described, a "kernel of infinite expansion" (qtd. in *English Composition as a Happening*).

SEAN ZIEBARTH, ENGLISH TEACHER,
FOUNTAIN VALLEY HIGH SCHOOL

DISCUSSION QUESTIONS

1. Think about the student voice hierarchy and your current context. Create a chart of examples of listening, collaboration, and leadership at your school or in your classroom. What minor shifts can be made?
2. Identify a content-driven unit that could be replaced by a design thinking, inquiry, or project-based learning approach. Who at your school or in your district can support you to make this shift?
3. Which of the ideas presented here resonate the most or might work in your context?
4. What courageous conversations about student voice and choice need to happen within your building or within your district?

CONCLUDING THOUGHTS

FROM THE STUDENT'S DESK: KAREN

My first blog post on my Medium profile is about how school made me fall out of love with reading. I wrote it for Mr. Ziebarth's English class. I was sixteen at the time, but that essay details how my unhappiness with school began way before I entered my junior year of high school. Shortly after that, I published another blog entitled "I'm a Loser Because of School," which was my submission for Mr. Ziebarth's Question Exploration assignment for the book we were reading: *The Catcher in the Rye*. I define what school is to me, why "I hate doing school things, but I love learning," and present a few solutions for the problems I experience in school. "I'm a Loser Because of School" was the product of student choice in the classroom and the foundation of this book that I began writing when I was seventeen. Twenty-year-old me is currently writing these concluding thoughts.

When I first started sharing my experiences as a student at sixteen, I really had no faith in the education system. I was burned out after so many years of schooling (dare I say early-onset senioritis?), unstimulated, stressed, and bored. This isn't to say that I think school is useless and shouldn't exist. I'd be nothing without school, especially as a first-generation student, and I'm lucky to have received a high-quality public K–12 education that prepared me to succeed in a traditional sense (i.e., attend college) since day one. But I still wondered if school could change for the better. I didn't think there were many people who were interested in reforming school or saw the problems I saw. I thought students would be stuck doing the same thing and suffering from the same issues for decades to come.

I hope it makes you happy to hear that over the years I've been working on this book with Jen, I've come to be more confident that school can become a better place for students because there are educators who have practices that prioritize a comfortable, welcoming, and empowering learning environment for students. I was excited every time I read about the steps and changes Jen created and adopted as a teacher and how these have made her classroom a better place for students. Several of the solutions Jen shared are things I didn't even know existed, like Minecraft in chapter 1 and class escape room games in chapter 3. Jen also mentioned that she discusses my ideas with her daughters and students and acts upon the feedback they give her, such as by adjusting assignment due dates and LMS notifications to decrease students' anxiety, as mentioned in chapter 4, which moved me because I saw firsthand how my perspective as a student has value. Likewise, when I read every teacher's contribution to this book, my pessimistic view of the school system gradually became less pessimistic. From Deanna Lough's single-point rubric in chapter 2 to Alex Valencic's homework menu in chapter 4, I saw how each educator's practices change their classrooms for the better, and I wished that I could've been their student for just one day. And now I'm in university, where there are so many opportunities to choose what and how you want to learn, to conduct your own research, and to advocate for students at the administrative level. I'm experiencing the most enriching side of education I've never experienced before and hope it can be tapped into at the K–12 level.

I know there are many, many teachers who strive to make school about learning and not about schooling—each in their own way, just as the teachers who've contributed to this book do. I also acknowledge that asking only educators to make changes is not enough to challenge and deconstruct the monolith of traditional schooling nor will it end serious issues teachers face, such as a lack of support from administration and low and unfair pay that pushes them out of education altogether.

Self-reflection was a critical part of writing this book. I thought a lot about what I'm like as a student, which has been shaped by the competitive schooling environment I grew up in. I thought about how a part of my negative experiences in school is my own opinions and attitudes, such as when I choose not to be engaged because I only want to do enough to get As. When I talk to students around me about changing school, they agree that school is more about schooling than about learning, but they don't have an interest in making these changes. After being conditioned to be good students our entire lives, we're used to how things are. We've internalized some negative beliefs about school, and we just want to get out as soon as we can. We don't know if school can be different from what it has been for the years and years we've been students. How can education be transformed when its primary beneficiaries can't imagine a different reality and are therefore hesitant to spearhead change?

This is why students need to have a voice from the very beginning—to actively participate in making decisions about their education, to learn that they are the most important people in school, and to be passionate about creating a better future for all. When the entire education system reflects on itself and puts students first, school can become the best place to learn.

FROM THE TEACHER'S DESK: JENNIFER

Writing this book together with Karen has been so very rewarding. Not only have I gotten to know a young woman who is bright and passionate, but her perspective has helped me to shine a light on my own practice and pushed my thinking.

Karen has pushed me to think of students who I think are navigating school effectively and thriving but who are in fact flailing.

Karen has pushed me to think of all of the students who may feel marginalized and who don't just need a content expert at the front of the room or a guide on the side, but someone who stands with them and prioritizes them over content.

Karen has pushed me to think about all of the antiquated practices we continue to do because we have always done them.

Karen has pushed me to think about how I can make greater connections to what I am teaching and the world in which we currently live.

Karen has pushed me to think about ways I can help my students become more autonomous and self-directed.

Karen began this book referencing Sir Ken Robinson's TED Talk, "Do Schools Kill Creativity?," which dates back to 2006. I remember the first time I watched it quite vividly. It made me laugh and it made me think, but it also made me very uncomfortable because I am a teacher who loves my students and wants school to be a place for them to be curious and empowered and to love learning. I am sad that we still aren't there, but I am very hopeful as well.

When we were forced into remote learning as a result of a pandemic, I thought that was the biggest disrupter to education—that when we went back to in-person learning, we would do so with fundamentally different priorities for what school should be. That was not the case, although we did see many teachers leave our noble profession. At the time of writing, people are speculating that AI is the biggest disrupter—that it will force us to think differently about our teaching and learning. And while I know that to be true to a great extent, I am wondering if the biggest disrupter to education may be a generation of students who refuse to do school the way it has been traditionally taught. Students have been ready to share their voices and perspectives for a long time now. Are we ready to listen?

ENDNOTES

INTRODUCTION

1. Ken Robinson, "Do Schools Kill Creativity?," 2006, https://www.ted.com/talks/sir_ken_robinson_do_schools_kill_creativity.
2. George Couros, "That Every Learner Feels Welcome in School: Hopes for School," in *The Innovator's Mindset Podcast*, March 9, 2019, https://youtu.be/RE4vXDK69jk?si=BuRJhcq0g1RfZlo_.

CHAPTER 1

1. Janet Metcalfe, "Learning from Errors," *Annual Review of Psychology* 68 (2017): 465–89.
2. Robert B. Reich, "One Education Does Not Fit All," *New York Times*, July 11, 2000, https://www.nytimes.com/2000/07/11/opinion/one-education-does-not-fit-all.html.
3. Karen Phan, "Classrooms Must Center around Humanity," Medium, January 31, 2021, https://zapkaren.medium.com/more-human-classrooms-e69c2ae0349b.
4. Erica Goldson, "Speech," America via Erica, June 5, 2010, http://americaviaerica.blogspot.com/p/speech.html.
5. One way to minimize regrading is to implement a policy where a regrade means you can either lose or gain points or get the same grade. One of my professors does this to encourage students to be mindful when they request a regrade because they could potentially lose points, so they'll only ask for one when they're confident that they should have earned more points. I think this is a fair policy.

6 Karen Phan, "Students Benefit More from Peer Reviewing than They Think They Do," Baron News, November 29, 2018, https://www.baronnews.com/2018/11/29/students-benefit-more-from-peer-reviewing-than-they-think-they-do/.

7 Margie Warrell, "Have You Learnt to Fail Forward? The Lesson We Can't Learn Soon Enough," *Forbes*, August 31, 2017, https://www.forbes.com/sites/margiewarrell/2017/08/31/why-schools-are-teaching-kids-to-fail/.

8 Lylyan Yenson, "Normalize Being Wrong," Baron News, November 8, 2020, https://www.baronnews.com/2020/11/08/normalize-being-wrong/.

9 Much of this section originally appeared on the author's blog at https://zapkaren.medium.com/im-a-loser-because-of-school-ed6dba01bb66.

10 Catlin Tucker, "Choice Boards: Benefits, Design Tips & Differentiation," August 16, 2021, https://catlintucker.com/2021/08/choice-boards101/.

11 John Hattie, *Visible Learning for Teachers: Maximizing Impact on Learning* (SAGE Publications, 2012), 251–252.

12 Oxford Teaching Ideas, "Peer Feedback," https://www.ctl.ox.ac.uk/peer-feedback.

13 Mari Venturino, "Peer Feedback with Forms," March 17, 2018, https://mariedublog.wordpress.com/2018/03/17/peer-feedback-with-forms/.

14 Mark Gardner, "Teaching Students to Give Peer Feedback," Edutopia, October 8, 2019, https://www.edutopia.org/article/teaching-students-give-peer-feedback/.

15 Garfield Gini-Newman, "Linking Creativity and Critical Thinking," Edmonton Regional Learning Consortium, April 2016, https://youtu.be/av6hQMNC5E4.

16 "Creativity: The Science Behind the Madness," Big Think, July 3, 2020, https://bigthink.com/neuropsych/brain-science-of-creativity/.

17 Ken Robinson, "Do Schools Kill Creativity," Ted Talk, 13:14, February 2006, https://www.ted.com/talks/sir_ken_robinson_do_schools_kill_creativity?utm_campaign=tedspread&utm_medium=referral&utm_source=tedcomshare.

18 Peter Liljedahl, Building Thinking Classrooms, https://www.buildingthinkingclassrooms.com/about-btc.

19 Chuck Wiederhold and Spencer Kagan, Cooperative Learning and Higher-Level Thinking: The Q-Matrix (Kagan Cooperative Learning, 1998).

20 Adapted from "My 2021 Failing Report," https://www.ajjuliani.com/blog/my-2021-failing-report.

CHAPTER 2

1 Alfie Kohn, "The Case against Grades," November 2011, https://www.alfiekohn.org/article/case-grades/.
2 "What's the Problem with Grades?" *IB Community Blog*, May 11, 2017, https://blogs.ibo.org/blog/2017/05/11/whats-the-problem-with-grades/.
3 Anne G. Wheaton, Sherry Everett Jones, Adina C. Cooper, and Janet B. Croft, "Short Sleep Duration among Middle School and High School Students—United States, 2015," *Morbidity and Mortality Weekly Report*, 67, no. 3 (January 2018): 85–90, https://www.cdc.gov/mmwr/volumes/67/wr/mm6703a1.htm?s_cid=mm6703a1_w.
4 Eric Suni, "Sleep for Teenagers," Sleep Foundation, updated October 4, 2023, https://www.sleepfoundation.org/teens-and-sleep.
5 Andrew Simmons, "Why Students Cheat—and What to Do about it," Edutopia, April 27, 2018, https://www.edutopia.org/article/why-students-cheat-and-what-do-about-it/; Samantha Selby, "Insights into How & Why Students Cheat at High-Performing Schools," Challenge Success, March 24, 2019, https://challengesuccess.org/resources/insights-into-how-why-students-cheat-at-high-performing-schools/.
6 Howie Hua (@howie_hua), "Ugh, I caught another student cheating on a test. Even having them sign an honor code saying they are only allowed to look at their notes and our videos, AND they can revise until they earn an A, I'm still not creating an environment where they can be honest with their work," Twitter, December 10, 2020, https://twitter.com/howie_hua/status/1337168761086865418?s=20.
7 Kohn, "The Case against Grades."
8 Vanessa Ellis, "Not Yet Gradeless, but Grading Less," Grow Beyond Grades, February 12, 2021, https://growbeyondgrades.org/blog/not-yet-gradeless-grading-less.
9 Andrew Burnett, "How to Create a Gradeless Math Classroom that Requires Grades," *7th Grade with Mr. Burnett*, March 8, 2018, https://burnettmath.wordpress.com/2018/03/08/how-to-create-a-gradeless-math-classroom-in-a-school-that-requires-grades/.

ENDNOTES

10 Abe Moore, "A Year of Mathematical Freedom: Replacing Stress and Conformity with Enjoyment and Creativity," Human Restoration Project, Medium, January 21, 2019, https://medium.com/human-restoration-project/a-year-of-mathematical-freedom-68c70e184b76.
11 Damian Cooper and Jeff Catania, *Because of a Teacher, Volume II: Stories from the First Years of Teaching*, edited by George Couros (IMPress, 2022).
12 *Growing Success: Assessment, Evaluation, and Reporting in Ontario Schools*, Ontario Ministry of Education, 2010, www.edu.gov.on.ca/eng/policyfunding/growsuccess.pdf.
13 "Effective Effort Rubric," https://www.mindsetworks.com/websitemedia/resources/effort-rubric-for-students.pdf.
14 Andrew shared a whole year of examples of his student navigation tool, which can be found at jcasatodd.com/book.

CHAPTER 3

1 "School Connectedness," American Psychological Association, 2014, https://www.apa.org/pi/lgbt/programs/safe-supportive/school-connectedness.
2 The Learning Network, "What Students Are Saying about Remote Learning," *New York Times*, April 9, 2020, https://www.nytimes.com/2020/04/09/learning/what-students-are-saying-about-remote-learning.html.
3 Monica Anderson, Michelle Faverio, and Colleen McClain, "How Teens Navigate School During COVID-19," Pew Research Center, June 2, 2022, https://www.pewresearch.org/internet/2022/06/02/how-teens-navigate-school-during-covid-19/.

   The report notes that roughly half or more teens reported feeling about as close to their classmates (52 percent) and teachers (58 percent) as they were before the pandemic.
4 Ellen McCarthy, "Teenagers during the Coronavirus Pandemic: The Loneliness of an Interrupted Adolescence," *Washington Post*, February 11, 2021, https://www.washingtonpost.com/lifestyle/style/teenagers-covid-pandemic-mental-health/2021/02/10/3389983a-39d6-11eb-9276-ae0ca72729be_story.html.
5 The Learning Network, "What Students Are Saying about Remote Learning."

6   Katelyn Nguyen, "FVHS Sees Rise in As and Fs after Full Semester of Distance Learning," Baron News, April 19, 2021, https://www.baronnews.com/2021/04/19/fvhs-sees-rise-in-as-and-fs-after-full-semester-of-distance-learning/.

7   Leah Shafer, "What Makes a Good School Culture?," Harvard Graduate School of Education, July 23, 2018, https://www.gse.harvard.edu/news/uk/18/07/what-makes-good-school-culture.

8   Kathryn C. Monahan, Sabrina Oesterle, and J. David Hawkins, "Predictors and Consequences of School Connectedness: The Case for Prevention," *Prevention Researcher* 17, no. 3 (September 2010): 3+, Gale OneFile: Health and Medicine, link.gale.com/apps/doc/A259750109/HRCA?u=anon~3a9374f9&sid=googleScholar&xid=05e60ad5.

9   Robert W. Blum, "A Case for School Connectedness," Docest, 2005, https://docest.com/a-case-for-school-connectedness.

10   Hugues Sampasa-Kanyinga, Jean-Philippe Chaput, and Hayley A. Hamilton, "Social Media Use, School Connectedness, and Academic Performance Among Adolescents," *Journal of Primary Prevention* 40 (2019): 189–211.

11   JaHun Kim, Elaine Walsh, Kenneth Pike, and Elaine A. Thompson, "Cyberbullying and Victimization and Youth Suicide Risk: The Buffering Effects of School Connectedness," *Journal of School Nursing* 36, no. 4 (2020): 251–257, http://doi.org/10.1177/1059840518824395.

12   "New CDC Data Illuminate Youth Mental Health Threats during the COVID-19 Pandemic," Centers for Disease Control and Prevention, March 31, 2022, https://www.cdc.gov/media/releases/2022/p0331-youth-mental-health-covid-19.html.

13   Sarah Schwartz, "Teachers Push for Books with More Diversity, Fewer Stereotypes," Education Week, June 11, 2019, https://www.edweek.org/teaching-learning/teachers-push-for-books-with-more-diversity-fewer-stereotypes/2019/06.

14   Rudine Sims Bishop, "Mirrors, Windows, and Sliding Glass Doors," *Perspectives* 1, no. 3 (1990): ix.

15   A how-to for creating a similar Google project can be found at jcasatodd.com.

16   Noa Daniel, "Play It Forward," TEDx Talk, February 2020, https://www.ted.com/talks/noa_daniel_play_it_forward.

17 Katie Martin, *Evolving Education: Shifting to a Learner-Centered Paradigm* (IMPress, 2021), 23.
18 CASEL, "What Does the Research Say?," https://casel.org/fundamentals-of-sel/what-does-the-research-say/.
19 CASEL, "What Is the CASEL Framework?," https://casel.org/fundamentals-of-sel/what-is-the-casel-framework/#the-casel-5.
20 A link to this and other templates can be found at jcasatodd.com.
21 A copy of a grade seven-to-twelve lesson with ideas for younger grades can be found at jcasatodd.com.

CHAPTER 4

1 Candy Schulman, "Burnt Out on the High School Treadmill," *Washington Post*, May 29, 2011, https://www.washingtonpost.com/opinions/burnout-on-the-high-school-treadmill/2011/05/27/AG7mTNEH_story.html.
2 Sonya Kulkarni and Pallavi Gorantla, "Students Spend Three Times Longer on Homework than Average, Survey Reveals," *Three Penny Press*, January 9, 2022, https://threepennypress.org/features/2022/01/09/homework-hours.
3 Valerie Strauss and Denise Pope, "Does Homework Work When Kids Are Learning All Day at Home?," *Washington Post*, September 1, 2020, https://www.washingtonpost.com/education/2020/09/01/does-homework-work-when-kids-are-learning-all-day-home/.
4 Janine Bempechat, "The Case for (Quality) Homework: Why It Improves Learning, and How Parents Can Help," *Education Next* 19, no. 1 (Winter 2019): 36+, Gale Academic OneFile, link.gale.com/apps/doc/A566264024/AONE?u=anon~f6d9c635&sid=googleScholar&xid=65ac8b43.
5 Susan M. Brookhart, *How to Give Effective Feedback to Your Students*, 2nd ed. (ASCD, 2017), 86, https://files.ascd.org/staticfiles/ascd/pdf/siteASCD/publications/books/How-to-Give-Effective-Feedback-to-Your-Students-2nd-Edition-sample-chapters.pdf.
6 Mary Davenport, "How to Improve Homework for This Year—and Beyond," Edutopia, December 16, 2020, https://www.edutopia.org/article/rethinking-homework-year-and-beyond/.
7 Want more? You can check out *Ditch That Homework* by Matt Miller and Alice Keeler, or go to efficienteach.com, a collection of teacher-suggested

practices to help you save time and teach better—which is at the heart of optimizing your instructional time!

CHAPTER 5

1. Lory Hough, "What's Worth Learning in School?," *Ed.*, January 10, 2015, https://www.gse.harvard.edu/news/ed/15/01/whats-worth-learning-school.
2. Next Gen Personal Finance, *NGFP's State of Financial Education Report*, 2022, https://d3f7q2msm2165u.cloudfront.net/aaa-content/user/files/Files/NGPFAnnualReport_2022.pdf.
3. Deloitte, *The Deloitte Global 2022 Gen Z and Millennial Survey*, 2022, https://www.deloitte.com/global/en/issues/work/genzmillennialsurvey-2022.html.
4. Elizabeth Marks et al., "Young People's Voices on Climate Anxiety, Government Betrayal, and Moral Injury: A Global Phenomenon," http://dx.doi.org/10.2139/ssrn.3918955.
5. World Economic Forum, "These Are 5 Skills Kids Will Need in the Future," September 22, 2022, https://www.weforum.org/videos/these-are-the-skills-kids-will-need-in-the-future.
6. Bernard Marr, "The Top 10 Most In-Demand Skills for the Next 10 Years," *Forbes*, October 12, 2022, www.forbes.com/sites/bernardmarr/2022/08/22/the-top-10-most-in-demand-skills-for-the-next-10-years/?sh=5c38bc8d17be.
7. "OECD Future of Education and Skills 2030/2040," OECD, 2022, https://www.oecd.org/education/2030-project/.
8. Adobe, "What Is Digital Literacy?," 2023, https://www.adobe.com/acrobat/hub/how-to/what-is-digital-literacy.
9. Daniel Herman, "The End of High-School English," *Atlantic*, December 9, 2022, https://www.theatlantic.com/technology/archive/2022/12/openai-chatgpt-writing-high-school-english-essay/672412/.
10. Dan Rosenzweig-Ziff, "New York City Blocks Use of the ChatGPT Bot in Its Schools," *Washington Post*, January 5, 2023, https://www.washingtonpost.com/education/2023/01/05/nyc-schools-ban-chatgpt/.
11. Lory Hough, "What's Worth Learning in School?"

ENDNOTES

12 "CIWM Presents Personal FinANTs," Center for Investment and Wealth Management, UC Irvine Paul Merage School of Business, https://merage.uci.edu/ciwm-events/personal-finants-home.html.

13 Kate Whiting, "These Are the Top 10 Job Skils of Tomorrow—and How Long It Takes to Learn Them," World Economic Forum, October 21, 2020, https://www.weforum.org/agenda/2020/10/top-10-work-skills-of-tomorrow-how-long-it-takes-to-learn-them/.

14 I read this in George Couros's blog at https://georgecouros.ca/blog/archives/13805.

15 John Hattie, *Visible Learning for Teachers: Maximizing Impact on Learning*.

16 A copy of this assignment can be found at jcasatodd.com with resources for this chapter.

17 "Expectations by Strand," Curriculum and Resources, Ontario Ministry of Education, https://www.dcp.edu.gov.on.ca/en/curriculum/elementary-language/grades/grade-8/strands.

18 Stephen Marche, "The College Essay Is Dead," *Atlantic*, December 6, 2022, https://www.theatlantic.com/technology/archive/2022/12/chatgpt-ai-writing-college-student-essays/672371/.

19 It is important to note the age restriction of these tools.

20 Alberta Education, "What is Literacy?," 2023, https://education.alberta.ca/literacy-and-numeracy/literacy/everyone/literacy-videos/.

21 David Sillito, "Teens Shun Traditional News Channels for TikTok and Instagram, Ofcom Says," BBC, July 20, 2022, https://www.bbc.com/news/entertainment-arts-62238307.

22 Denise Hattwig et al., "ACRL Visual Literacy Competency Standards for Higher Education," American Library Association, 2011, https://www.ala.org/acrl/standards/visualliteracy.

23 American Library Association, "Digital Literacy, Libraries, and Public Policy," January 2013, http://hdl.handle.net/11213/16261.

24 I have included several digital literacy resources at jcasatodd.com in the resources for this chapter.

25 "Our School," Gibson Ek High School, 2023, https://gibsonek.isd411.org/our-school.

26 This template can be found at jcasatodd.com with the resources for this chapter.

27 A copy of Melisa's projects can be accessed with the resources for this chapter.

CHAPTER 6

1 Dana L. Mitra, "Amplifying Student Voice," ASCD PD Online, https://pdo.ascd.org/LMSCourses/PD11OC100M/media/RTI_M05_Reading_04_Amplifying_Student_Voice.pdf.
2 Harvard Business Publishing, "Why Your Students Are Disengaged," August 3, 2022, https://hbsp.harvard.edu/inspiring-minds/why-your-students-are-disengaged.
3 Tom Sherrington, "Myth: Teacher-Led Instruction and Student-Centred Learning Are Opposites," Teacherhead, December 8, 2019, https://teacherhead.com/2019/12/08/myth-teacher-led-instruction-and-student-centred-learning-are-opposites/.
4 Sherrington, "Myth."
5 Joshua Dantzler, "A Student's View: Young People Are the Biggest Stakeholders in Any School. They Deserve a Seat at the Decision-Making Table," The 74, November 10, 2019, https://www.the74million.org/article/a-students-view-young-people-are-the-biggest-stakeholder-in-any-school-they-deserve-a-seat-at-the-decisionmaking-table/.
6 Anneliese Duong, "FVHS's Third House of Representatives Meeting to Address More of Students' Concerns," Baron News, March 19, 2022, https://www.baronnews.com/2022/03/19/third-house-of-reps-recap/.
7 Dana Mitra, "Student Voice in Secondary Schools: The Possibility for Deeper Change," *Journal of Educational Administration* 56, no. 5 (2018): 473–487.
8 See https://jcasatodd.com/making-learning-real-and-relevant-student-voice-in-action/.
9 PBLWorks, "What Is PBL?," https://www.pblworks.org/what-is-pbl?gclid=CjwKCAiA5Y6eBhAbEiwA_2ZWlavSWWq8VYIqtpS0O-YLggycKmz2B-5uFs45pfH4QcSK0MRtMzYmehoCKu0QAvD_BwE.
10 Centre for Teaching and Learning, "Inquiry-Based Learning," Queen's University,https://www.queensu.ca/ctl/resources/instructional-strategies/inquiry-based-learning.
11 Cornelius Minor, *We Got This: Equity, Access, and the Quest to Be Who Our Students Need Us To Be* (Heinemann, 2019).

12 Minor, *We Got This*, 17.
13 America's Promise Alliance, "All of Who I Am: Perspectives from Young People about Social, Emotional, and Cognitive Learning," Summer 2020, https://americaspromise.org/wp-content/uploads/pdf/HLH_report_online.pdf.
14 If you teach middle or elementary school, your local high school likely has an interior design class to tap into.
15 You can find a more detailed breakdown of this assignment at bit.ly/BOLDqft.

ACKNOWLEDGMENTS

KAREN

Thank you to my family, friends, teachers, and professors for their continued investment in my curiosity and learning.

Thank you to the California public school and public library systems for providing me with an excellent and life-changing education. I attribute many of my accomplishments to the education I have received. I would be nothing without school.

Thank you to Jennifer and the IMPress team for supporting student agency and learning.

JENNIFER

I would like to firstly thank Karen for sharing her story with me and the world. Getting to know you has been a blessing; it has been a long road but worth it to see the culmination of all of that hard work in the form of this book!

I would like to acknowledge and thank George Couros who not only introduced me to Karen and this project but who has also inspired me for over a decade. Thanks, George, for pushing me to take risks and believing I could be an author. I am forever grateful.

Thank you Paige Couros for being so incredible in every way, every step of the way. Thank you to the team at IMPress, especially Sal and Lindsey for your suggestions, edits and expertise.

ACKNOWLEDGMENTS

Thank you to the incredible educators who lent their voices to this book in the form of idea spotlights. We are so appreciative of your time, effort, and contributions.

To my daughters, Sydney and Kelsey, whom I love with all my heart, thank you for your support, opinions and encouragement and for always keeping me in check.

To my husband, Stewart, thank you for allowing me the freedom to work on my passion projects; my achievements are a direct result of your love and support.

To all of the educators, in every role, for your unwavering dedication, your endless patience, and your tireless efforts to inspire and empower the next generation of students.

ABOUT THE AUTHORS

KAREN PHAN

Karen Phan is a product of the California K-12 and University of California public school systems. During her undergraduate education, she studied English and human-computer interaction, two disciplines that taught her about vibrant human experiences and the power of storytelling to amplify diverse voices. Karen is a first-generation student who is passionate about learning. In her free time, she enjoys doing arts and crafts, hiking, reading, and rewatching her favorite childhood movies.

JENNIFER CASA-TODD

Jennifer Casa-Todd is a wife, mom, educator, former literacy consultant, and the author of several books focusing on digital leadership. Jennifer was the recipient of the YSCPC Teaching Excellence Award (2023) and the ISTE Digital Citizenship Network Award (2020). She is an Ontario Google Educator Group leader, a Google Certified Innovator, and a board member of the Canadian Library Association. Jennifer has a masters in education with a specialization in curriculum and technology. Jennifer can currently be found supporting preservice teachers at Lakehead University, traveling, golfing, curling, or reading. She has been a presenter, featured speaker, and keynote speaker at conferences across Canada, the US, and virtually around the world. She has contributed to several other books and has published peer-reviewed articles around a variety of topics including education, student voice, and digital leadership. Jennifer is passionate about amplifying the voices of students as well as showing teachers and students how they can use technology positively and productively. Learn more about her at jcasatodd.com.

MORE FROM IMPRESS

Empower: What Happens When Students Own Their Learning by A.J. Juliani and John Spencer

Learner-Centered Innovation: Spark Curiosity, Ignite Passion, and Unleash Genius by Katie Martin

Unleash Talent: Bringing Out the Best in Yourself and the Learners You Serve by Kara Knollmeyer

Reclaiming Our Calling: Hold On to the Heart, Mind, and Hope of Education by Brad Gustafson

Take the L.E.A.P.: Ignite a Culture of Innovation by Elisabeth Bostwick

Drawn to Teach: An Illustrated Guide to Transforming Your Teaching written by Josh Stumpenhorst and illustrated by Trevor Guthke

Math Recess: Playful Learning in an Age of Disruption by Sunil Singh and Dr. Christopher Brownell

Innovate inside the Box: Empowering Learners through UDL and the Innovator's Mindset by George Couros and Katie Novak

Personal & Authentic: Designing Learning Experiences That Last a Lifetime by Thomas C. Murray

Learner-Centered Leadership: A Blueprint for Transformational Change in Learning Communities by Devin Vodicka

Kids These Days: A Game Plan for (Re)Connecting with Those We Teach, Lead, & Love by Dr. Jody Carrington

MORE FROM IMPRESS

UDL and Blended Learning: Thriving in Flexible Learning Landscapes
by Katie Novak and Catlin Tucker

Teachers These Days: Stories & Strategies for Reconnection
by Dr. Jody Carrington and Laurie McIntosh

Because of a Teacher: Stories of the Past to Inspire the Future of Education
written and curated by George Couros

Because of a Teacher, Volume 2: Stories from the First Years of Teaching
written and curated by George Couros

Evolving Education: Shifting to a Learner-Centered Paradigm
by Katie Martin

Adaptable: How to Create an Adaptable Curriculum and Flexible Learning Experiences That Work in Any Environment by A.J. Juliani

Lead from Where You Are: Building Intention, Connection, and Direction in Our Schools by Joe Sanfelippo

The Shift to Student-Led: Reimagining Classroom Workflows with UDL and Blended Learning by Catlin R. Tucker & Katie Novak

The Design Thinking Classroom: Using Design Thinking to Reimagine the Role and Practice of Educators by David Jakes

Shift Writing into the Classroom with UDL and Blended Learning
by Catlin R. Tucker and Katie Novak

Teach Happy: Small Steps to Big Joy by Kim Strobel

What Makes a Great Principal by George Couros and Allyson Apsey

www.ingramcontent.com/pod-product-compliance
Lightning Source LLC
Chambersburg PA
CBHW050552160426
43199CB00015B/2631